GET A GRIP!

A Year 'Round
Drama-Rama
of Scenes and Monologs
for Christian Teens

L.G. ENSCOE
and
ANNIE ENSCOE

Foreword by Tim Hansel

MERIWETHER PUBLISHING LTD.
Colorado Springs, Colorado

Meriwether Publishing Ltd., Publisher
Box 7710
Colorado Springs, CO 80933

Editor: Arthur L. Zapel
Typesetting: Sharon E. Garlock
Cover design: Tom Myers
Cover photograph: Tim Down

© Copyright MCMXCI Meriwether Publishing Ltd.
Printed in the United States of America
First Edition

Library of Congress Cataloging-in-Publication Data

Enscoe, Lawrence G.
    Get a grip! : a year 'round drama-rama of scenes and monologs for
  Christian teens / by Lawrence Enscoe & Andrea Enscoe.
      p.   cm.
    Summary: A collection of short contemporary Christian dramas, covering
such topics as surviving the teen years, overcoming addictions, and trusting
God.
    ISBN 0-916260-82-8 : $9.95
    1. Young adult drama, American. 2. Christian drama, American.
[1. Christian life--Drama. 2. Plays.] I. Enscoe, Andrea J.
II. Title.
PS3555.N74G47   1991
812'.54--dc20
                                          91-37422
                                               CIP
                                              AC

*This book is
dedicated to those
beleaguered,
hardworking,
indispensable
folks
known as*

CHURCH YOUTH WORKERS

(you know who you are)

TABLE OF CONTENTS

SECTION THREE
HOLIDAYS

NOTE: The numerals running vertically down the left margin of each page of dialogue are for the convenience of the director. With these, he/she may easily direct attention to a specific passage.

FOREWORD

After 30 years of youth work, I believe the material in *Get a Grip!* is some of the freshest, most ingenious, life-changing curriculum available. It's the best work of its kind for getting kids to participate and to dialog — two things youth ministry is all about.

Everything you need is here. The sketches are short, simple — but not simplistic — provocative and to the point. They've been written in such a way that anybody could use them. You don't have to be an actor or have training to perform any of them.

The material you will find inside these covers is creative, vital, on target — and much needed. They're relevant and appropriate to age group and language. And they can be used any time, any place, by anyone.

I wish their work could be found in every youth group in every church in the country. It would give youth groups a valid and vivid tool for asking the challenging questions.

We need more.

TIM HANSEL

Million-selling author of
When I Relax I Feel Guilty
and **Holy Sweat**

Founder and President of Summit Expedition

THE CHRISTIAN LIFE

Love Letters

*A Monolog on
Jesus' Love*

Anne Pirio in *Love Letters*.
(Glendale Presbyterian Church Youth Drama Team)

PRODUCTION NOTES

Love Letters can be used during the Easter season or as part of a study on Scriptures such as John 3:16, John 15:12, 5:2 or Romans 5:6-8.

CAST: PAIGE WESLEY, a teenage girl.

SCENE: A bedroom. The present.

RUNNING TIME: Four to five minutes.

COSTUME NOTE: Casual.

PROPS: Box or trunk, books, magazines, small box, letters, stuffed animals, Walkman.

1   *AT RISE:*   Loud dance music. PAIGE WESLEY comes in, dressed
2   in hang-around-the-house clothes. She's carrying a trunk or box
3   and listening to her Walkman, bopping. Sits down, opens the
4   trunk and starts pulling things out — stuffed animals,
5   magazines, books, etc. Looks at them and tosses them aside.
6   She looks up, sees the audience, smiles. Goes back to her work.
7   Suddenly, she whips her head back up, looking freaked out.
8   Rips off her headphones. The music halts. She smiles weakly.
9

10   **PAIGE:**   **Uh ... hi.** *(She gets it together.)* **I have this quirk.**
11   **This ... this thing I do.** *(Laughs.)* **Well, I know it's way**
12   **strange, but ... oh, yeah, hi, I'm Paige Wesley. Anyways,**
13   **I guess I'll tell you about it. Wait a second.** *(She starts*
14   *digging through the box, throwing stuff over her shoulder.)*
15   **Sorry. My room's a pig sty. Hold on a sec.** *(She finds what*
16   *she wants, a banged-up metal box with a lock on it. "Stay Out*
17   *and This Means You!" written on top.)*
18   **Well, this is it.** *(Opens the metal box.)* **This is what I**
19   **do.** *(Pulls out a handful of letters — creased, folded, taped, torn.*
20   *Some covered in hearts, lipstick kisses, Xs, Os, etc.)*
21   **I ... I collect love letters. Bizarre, huh? I started in**
22   **the seventh grade and I can't stop. When letters get**
23   **passed across the class, their last stop is me. Wailing**
24   **freshmen tear 'em up and toss 'em in the wastebasket? I**
25   **fish 'em out and tape 'em up.** *(Holds up a bunch tied with*
26   *ribbon. The sarcasm starts peeking through.)*
27   **Look at these. My favorite in the collection. The love**
28   **letters to Joanie Buckwood. The whole ninth grade**
29   **worth. I paid twenty bucks for it. Six different guys!**
30   **She was phenomenal!** *(Tosses the stack on the ground.)* **You**
31   **learn so much about human nature in these letters. Oh,**
32   **the power and fragileness of love. The passion and deeds**
33   **of attraction. The poetry of the human heart! Here's one.**
34   *(Adopts a "dude" attitude. Reads:)*
35   **"Yo, Pookie. Thanks for doin' my algebra homework**

1   all last semester. You're a way cool babe. Totally stay
2   that way. Love, Rodney. P.S. Love your figures!"
3   *(Clutching the letter to her)* **Gosh! I bet they get married!**
4   **Rodney and Pookie. Think of all that math homework**
5   **together!** *(Tosses it. Looks through the box.)* **Oh, here's a**
6   **pretty good one. Whoa, two lipstick lips, fifteen Xs, twelve**
7   **Os, one "Sealed with a Kiss" and hearts all around the**
8   **border. Must've taken her all of her English class to do**
9   **this.** *(Gets all prissy. Reads:)*
10   **"Dearest Mark. To love you as I do now, I must have**
11   **loved you forever.** *(She flashes a "gag me" look.)* **Everything**
12   **I see, even though I've seen it a million times, is fresh**
13   **and new because I have you in my life.** *(She looks sick.)* **I**
14   **will only ever love you, my snookums. Hope I can see you**
15   **after Mr. Puchalski's class today. Love, Kelley."** *(Tosses it.*
16   *Digs out another.)*
17   **Oh, yeah, this one's a killer.** *(A nasally geek. Falls to*
18   *her knees and reads.)*
19   **"Oh, Michelle. I would do *anything* for you. I would**
20   **buy you *anything*. Go *anywhere*! Be *anyone*! You are the**
21   **captain of this shipwrecked heart.** *(She gags.)* **I would give**
22   ***anything* to make you happy. Please say you like me. I**
23   ***need* you. Love, Marlin. P.S. Wanna borrow my Michael**
24   **Jackson CDs?"**
25   **Way incredible, huh? They went out exactly twice.**
26   **She thought he was a total geek. She kept the CDs. Too**
27   **bad. Marlin's an OK guy.** *(She whips through the letters,*
28   *pulling out ones here and there.)* **Oh, there're some winners**
29   **in here, lemme tell you. Everybody talking about**
30   **"forever" and "everlasting" and what they really mean**
31   **is . . . a semester. Talking about love and passion, until**
32   **one of 'em does something the other doesn't like. I mean,**
33   **come on, when're people gonna wake up and get it.**
34   **Nobody loves you totally and forever. Nobody.** *(She*
35   *sarcastically reads through several, tossing them on the ground.)*

1   **"I'll always love you, forever." "I don't know how I**
2   **can live another minute without you"** — oh, puhleeeze!
3   **"You're the greatest thing that's ever happened to me!"**
4   **"I will never leave you or forsake you!"** *(Stops.)* **I don't**
5   **remember that one.** *(She picks up the last one and scans*
6   *through it. She reads:)*
7   **"I loved you first. I loved you before you even knew**
8   **who I was. I have given all for you — everything I have.**
9   **I want to fill your heart with myself. My love doesn't see**
10 **what you have done, only who you are. Will you think**
11 **about me? I'll be waiting."**
12   **Get real! Who's this to?** *(Flips to the first page.)* **Paige**
13 **Wesley? It's to me.** *(Starting to freak)* **Get out, I don't**
14 **remember anyone ever . . . no one's ever written me**
15 **a . . . wait! This is a joke. It has to be a joke. No one's ever**
16 **written me a love letter. No one even knows I'm alive!**
17 *(Flips through the pages.)* **Who wrote this?! There're no**
18 **hearts, no Xs, no Os. What's this red stuff? Lipstick?**
19 *(Touches the page.)* **Somebody bled on this!** *(She turns to the*
20 *last page. Reads. Sits. Short pause.)*
21   **Love, Jesus.** *(Slow fade to blackout.)*
22
23
24
25
26
27
28
29
30
31
32
33
34
35

The Great SAT of Life

A Sketch on Trusting God

PRODUCTION NOTES

This sketch can be used for a discussion or talk about trusting God in times of uncertainty or confusion. It's based on Proverbs 3:5,6 and Psalms 62:8.

CAST: VOICE, SHIRLEY NEW-AGE, TINA TIMID, KEN CHECK-OUT, CARL CHEATER, CHRIS.

SCENE: A school auditorium. The present.

COSTUME NOTE: Modern, hip.

RUNNING TIME: Four to five minutes.

PROPS: Chairs, pencils, test booklets, cellular phone, a crystal, mirror, chalkboard.

1   *AT RISE:*   Five anxious students sitting in chairs. TINA TIMID,
2   SHIRLEY NEW-AGE, CARL CHEATER, KEN CHECKOUT,
3   and CHRIS. A chalkboard behind them reads, "The Great SAT
4   of Life — No Talking." The students are all talking. An Off-
5   stage VOICE is heard.)
6
7   **VOICE: Good morning! Welcome, students, to the Great**
8   **SAT of Life. There will be no talking, eating or drinking**
9   **during the test. Please fill in the bubble with a number**
10   **two pencil. Fill in the bubble completely. Don't take too**
11   **long on each question. Remember, you only have seventy**
12   **to eighty years to complete the test. You may turn your**
13   **books over now.** *(They turn their books over. A collective*
14   *groan.)*
15   **ALL: I *should'a studied more!***
16   **VOICE:** *(Off-stage)* **Shhhhhh!** *(They read the test. CHEATER rolls*
17   *back his pant leg and reads notes. NEW-AGE closes her eyes*
18   *and puts the test down. CHRIS watches her.)*
19   **CHRIS:** *(To NEW-AGE)* **Why aren't you working on the test?**
20   **NEW-AGE: What test? There is no test. I'm in an out-of-body**
21   **experience right now. My soul is astral traveling. My**
22   **crystal is warm. There is no test.**
23   **CHRIS: It's on the desk. Right in front of you.**
24   **NEW-AGE:** *(Chanting)* **There is no test ... there is no test ...**
25   **there is no —** *(CHRIS holds the test in front of her face.)* **Oh,**
26   **that test.** *(She smirks and starts reading. CHEATER has slid*
27   *off his belt and is reading notes on the backside. TINA looks*
28   *around and pulls out a portable phone stuffed in her purse.)*
29   **TINA:** *(Whispered)* **Mom, I don't have any of the answers. Help**
30   **me, will you, please? I can't do it alone.**
31   **VOICE: Shhhhhh!** *(CHRIS looks at CHECKOUT, sitting with*
32   *arms folded and looking ahead.)*
33   **NEW-AGE:** *(To CHECKOUT)* **Are you looking for your center?**
34   **CHECKOUT: Get over it. I'm just not takin' the stupid test.**
35   **NEW-AGE: If you could only find your chakras, you'd be able to —**

1   CHECKOUT: Get out of my face, crystal head! I'm not takin'
2   the stupid test because nobody's got any answers, all
3   right? It's all a major waste'a time. Even if ya come up
4   with an answer and filled in the dorky little bubble, it's
5   really just their opinion, right? Nobody knows anything.
6   Got any smoke on ya? *(NEW-AGE shakes her head.*
7   *CHEATER peels back the collar of the person in front of him*
8   *and reads. TINA dials another number.)*
9   TINA: *(Into the phone)* Hello, Ms. Landers. This is Tina. Tina
10   from your history class! Yeah. See, I'm not ready for this
11   test. Can you give me some of the answers? I
12   mean . . . could you just take the test for me? *(NEW-AGE*
13   *looks at CHRIS, whose eyes are closed in prayer.)*
14   NEW-AGE: Oh! You're finding your center!
15   CHRIS: No. My place.
16   NEW-AGE: Well, your place is the center! The center of
17   everything. You are everything, and everything is you.
18   Want my crystals?
19   CHRIS: I'm not meditating. I'm praying. *(The magic word.*
20   *Everybody turns and looks at CHRIS.)*
21   CHECKOUT: You mean, like, to God, dude? Give it up. No
22   answers there. One-sided conversation.
23   NEW-AGE: Well, that's kind of like meditating.
24   CHEATER: You think he's got Cliffs Notes?
25   TINA: You got his phone number?
26   VOICE: *(Off-stage)* **Shhhhhh!** *(They go back to work. NEW-AGE*
27   *holds a crystal to her forehead. CHRIS goes back to prayer. TINA*
28   *dials another number.)*
29   TINA: *(Into the phone)* Hello, can you put me through to Mr.
30   Wizard? *(CHEATER holds up a mirror, trying to see the test*
31   *behind him.)*
32   CHECKOUT: *(Grabbing the mirror)* Dude! Bonus! I need that a
33   sec!
34   CHRIS: God, I don't know all the answers. I know some of
35   these. I read up all I could. I went to the studies and all.

1   It's . . . well, some of these questions I just don't know.
2   They weren't in any of the books. Some of 'em I just don't
3   understand.
4   ·TINA: *(Into the phone)* **Can you put me through to the**
5   **Mahareeshi Yogibeary?** *(CHEATER pulls a piece of paper*
6   *out of his nose and reads it. Behind him, CHECKOUT sneezes.)*
7   NEW-AGE: *(Coming out of her trance)* **The Lifeforce bless you.**
8   CHECKOUT: **Get a life, Shirley MacLaine.**
9   NEW-AGE: **How about two?** *(She goes back into her meditation.)*
10   CHRIS: **God, you know how I'm feeling. I wanna do the right**
11   **thing. None of these people around here are getting**
12   **anywhere on this test. They don't have any answers. Mr.**
13   **Checkout over there doesn't even think there *are* any**
14   **answers. This guy over here's stealing the answers**
15   **nobody else even has. She's callin' everyone in town**
16   **hoping someone will do everything for her. And the New-**
17   **Age Queen over here, she . . . she doesn't even know she's**
18   **on the planet.** *(He sighs. Nods his head.)* **I'm just gonna**
19   **start. That's all. I'm gonna pick up this pencil and lean**
20   **on you.**
21   NEW-AGE: **There is no test . . . there is no test . . . I float on**
22   **clouds of warm liquid . . . no test . . . no test . . .**
23   CHECKOUT: **No answers, dude. No answers. Anybody got**
24   **any Jack Daniels around here?**
25   TINA: *Whaddaya mean Mother Theresa won't take a collect*
26   *call?*
27   VOICE: *(Off)* **Shhhhhh!** *(CHEATER takes off his shoe and reads*
28   *his foot.)*
29   CHRIS: **Thanks for my brains . . . and my common sense. And**
30   **your help.** *(CHRIS picks up his pencil and starts working. The*
31   *others stay in their bits as the lights go to blackout.)*
32
33
34
35

Perfect for the Job

A Sketch on Grace

PRODUCTION NOTES

Perfect for the Job can be used for teaching on grace and God's pure acceptance — or during job hunting seminars.

CAST: GRACE, a job interviewer; COURTNEY VANCE, a teen job interviewee.

SCENE: A personnel office. The present.

COSTUME NOTE: Modern, professional.

RUNNING TIME: Five minutes.

PROPS: Chairs, a chalkboard, papers, files, a clipboard.

1   *AT RISE:* A line of chairs. A chalkboard that reads "Interviews
2   Here." GRACE sits with a clipboard on her lap. She's shuffling
3   through papers. COURTNEY VANCE comes in, dressed tweedy
4   and carrying a file.
5

6   **COURTNEY:** *(Calling off)* **Through here?** *(Sees GRACE.)* **Oh,**
7   **I see. Thanks.** *(She goes to GRACE.)* **I'm here for the job.**
8   *(Fishes out a paper.)* **Here's my resumé. It was done on a**
9   **Macintosh. Laserjet printed.** *(Taps the paper.)* **Linen**
10   **finish.**
11   **GRACE:** *(Smiles)* **Very impressive, ah** . . . *(Reads resumé.)* . . .
12   **Courtney.**
13   **COURTNEY:** *(Beaming)* **Thanks.** *(Pause. COURTNEY stands*
14   *there.)*
15   **GRACE: Ah, you can just have a seat over there. I'll call you**
16   **when I'm ready for you.**
17   **COURTNEY: Oh.** *(Disappointed)* **Fine. I'll just** . . . **be sitting**
18   **over here.** *(She sits. Notices the audience. Leans in.)* **I'm not,**
19   **like, trying to sound all uppity or anything, but I'm a**
20   **shoo-in for this. It's true. I'm perfect for the job. Well, I've**
21   **worked hard to build up a resumé like that. Took all the**
22   **right courses — aced 'em all, too. Extra-curricular stuff.**
23   **I deserve this position. No really.**
24   **GRACE: Courtney Vance?**
25   **COURTNEY:** *(To the audience as she goes to GRACE)* **Great**
26   **resumé, too. Macintosh, Laserjet printed. Linen finish**
27   **paper. Perfect.**
28   **GRACE: Hello, Courtney. I'm Grace.** *(COURTNEY grabs her*
29   *hand and pumps it.)* **Yes. Well, please sit down.** *(COURTNEY*
30   *does.)* **Well, I have to tell you, this is really an incredible**
31   **resumé.** *(COURTNEY flashes a smile at the audience. She*
32   *mouths the word "perfect.")* **I don't think I've seen one better.**
33   **Three point nine GPA. Ninety-eighth percentile SAT**
34   **scores. Captain of the debating team. Student body**
35   **president. Block letters in track, swimming and golf.**

1   French, Spanish, Russian and Mandarin Chinese. Church
2   youth group leader. Honor roll all four years. Type eighty
3   words per minute. Scholarship awards. Your parents
4   must be very proud of you.
5   COURTNEY: Thank you. Yes, they are. I've made sure of it.
6   GRACE: I'm sure you have. Do you mind if I ask you a few
7   questions?
8   COURTNEY: Please.
9   GRACE: Fine. *(Pulls up her clipboard.)* Can you work full-time?
10   Thirty-two to forty hours a week?
11   COURTNEY: Yes I can.
12   GRACE: *(Makes a check on the application.)* Uh-huh. Ah, are you
13   available nights and weekends?
14   COURTNEY: Absolutely.
15   GRACE: *(Makes a check.)* Uh-huh. Do you have your own car?
16   COURTNEY: Yes I do.
17   GRACE: *(Checks)* Uh-huh. Any disabilities that might hinder
18   you on the job?
19   COURTNEY: None.
20   GRACE: *(Checks)* Are you currently under a doctor's care?
21   COURTNEY: No.
22   GRACE: *(Checks)* Have you ever lied to your mother?
23   COURTNEY: What?
24   GRACE: Have you ever lied to your mother?
25   COURTNEY: I . . . don't understand.
26   GRACE: Have you ever lied to your mother, Courtney?
27   COURTNEY: Ah . . . I don't know . . . I might . . . I think I
28   was out late once and I . . . I might have said I —
29   GRACE: True or false!
30   COURTNEY: True!
31   GRACE: *(Checks)* Uh-huh.
32   COURTNEY: What has that got to do with —?
33   GRACE: Have you ever cheated on a test?
34   COURTNEY: No way! Never ever, never ever!
35   GRACE: Never ever, never?

1   COURTNEY: Well . . . once when I was in the —

2   GRACE: *(Checks)* Uh-huh.

3   COURTNEY: Hold on! It was in the fourth grade. I was only

4   nine years old!

5   GRACE: Courtney, have you ever spit on your geeky little

6   brother's tuna sandwich before giving it to him?

7   COURTNEY: *(Suspicious)* Wait a minute! How'd you know I —

8   GRACE: *(Checks)* Uh-huh.

9   COURTNEY: Time out! *Time out!* What does that prove?!

10   GRACE: I'm sorry, Courtney. I'm afraid you're not perfect.

11   COURTNEY: But I *am perfect!* I'm perfect for the job!

12   GRACE: Well, according to these answers —

13   COURTNEY: Well, OK, so maybe I'm not perfectly perfect,

14   OK?! C'mon, then nobody's perfect, OK. If I'm not, nobody

15   is! Look, I spit on little Frankie's sandwich because he

16   flushed my Care Bear down the toilet. You can't crash

17   me out for that! *(She jumps to her feet, losing it.)* This is

18   insane! I've worked my rear off! That's killer stuff you've got

19   in front of you! I'm the pick of the crop! I'm the crème de la

20   crème! *Everybody says so!* *(Starts to cry.)* But . . . I worked

21   so hard . . . I worked so . . . OK, fine . . . I'll . . . I'll just —

22   GRACE: Relax, Courtney. You've got the job.

23   COURTNEY: How'm I going to tell my mother?! She's gonna

24   tear my — I what?

25   GRACE: You've got the job.

26   COURTNEY: I've got the job?!

27   GRACE: I never said you didn't get the job.

28   COURTNEY: *(Suspicious)* What did I do to deserve this?

29   GRACE: Nothing. You didn't do a thing.

30   COURTNEY: What? *(She sits.)* That's a switch.

31   GRACE: *(Holds up the resumé.)* This doesn't count, understand?

32   Nothing you ever did counts here. You're in here on my

33   word only. *(Tears up the resumé.)* This resumé is history,

34   OK? Do you still want the job?

35   COURTNEY: Let me get this straight. I'm going to have to be

1   **perfect from now on out, right?**

2   **GRACE:**   **Well, you can try. But you won't be. You've got the**

3   **job either way.** *(Pause)*

4   **COURTNEY:**   **When do you want me to start?**

5   **GRACE:**   **Immediately.**

6   **COURTNEY:**   *(A beat, then a smile)* **I'm in.** *(COURTNEY pumps*

7   *GRACE's hand as before. The lights fade to blackout.)*

8

9

10

11

12

13

14

15

16

17

18

19

20

21

22

23

24

25

26

27

28

29

30

31

32

33

34

35

The Very Least

*A Mime Parable
on Giving*

PRODUCTION NOTES

The Very Least can be used to talk about the Christian's role in helping the needy, in planning a social outreach program, or in discussion with Scriptures like Matthew 25:31-46, Luke 14:12-14 or Hebrews 13:16.

Can be performed indoors or as street theatre.

CAST: NEEDYDUDE, PREACH, CAL Q. LATER, DOE NATION.

SCENE: A city street. The present.

COSTUME NOTE: Modern.

RUNNING TIME: Four to five minutes.

PROPS: Chair, acting block, or crate; jacket with Christian buttons; muffler; stocking cap; Bible; squirt gun; checkbook; wallets; calculator; offering can; wallet pictures; cash; drum.

1   *AT RISE:*   Lights. The playing area is empty, except for an acting
2   block or crate. The sounds of a busy street, then softly a drum
3   begins to beat a steady cadence (this builds during the scene).
4
5   **NEEDYDUDE comes in, looks around. He's wearing**
6   **dirty, baggy clothes, disheveled. He sits on the block,**
7   **tired, hungry and dejected. He shivers from the cold.**
8   **PREACH comes in, falls into a march around the**
9   **block in rhythm with the drumbeat. He's wearing a heavy**
10   **jacket with lots of Christian buttons, sayings and**
11   **symbols — also, a warm muffler and stocking cap. He**
12   **preaches from a huge black Bible, admonishing and**
13   **gesturing.**
14   **The street sounds fade out.**
15   **NEEDYDUDE sees PREACH and is delighted. He**
16   **pulls out his pockets and holds out a hand. PREACH**
17   **doesn't see him, knocks past. NEEDYDUDE spins and**
18   **falls to the floor. He gets up, shakes off, goes to PREACH**
19   **again, shivering and asking for the scarf. Gets knocked**
20   **down again.**
21   **CAL Q. LATER comes in, dressed in a business suit**
22   **and balancing his checkbook with a calculator. CAL falls**
23   **in step behind PREACH.**
24   **NEEDYDUDE smiles and stands. He shows his**
25   **pockets to CAL. Then his empty wallet, pointing at the**
26   **moth that flies out. CAL brushes past NEEDYDUDE, who**
27   **topples to the floor as before.**
28   **DOE NATION comes in, dressed officiously and**
29   **carrying an offering can that reads, "God Cares." She**
30   **falls in step around the circle with the others.**
31   **NEEDYDUDE jumps up and reads the can. He**
32   **smiles, claps his hands, and goes to her. Points to the**
33   **can. She knocks into him without noticing. He tumbles down.**
34   **NEEDYDUDE stands, upset. Brushes off. He feels a**
35   **hunger pang and doubles over. He looks over at the three,**

1 marching in cadence, faster and faster. He shivers. He
2 goes to the circle, pointing to his wallet, his empty
3 pockets. He cradles a baby. He shows pictures. All the
4 while, he's dodging them as he steps in front of their
5 undaunted stride. He kneels down to beg them, but
6 scrambles out of the path of one, only to crawl into the
7 path of another. He finally escapes the vicious circle.
8   NEEDYDUDE is desperate. Stands on the block.
9 Waves for their attention. Nothing. Jumps up and down.
10 Does a little dance. No go. He pretends to be hanging
11 himself. No one bats an eye.
12   He looks down. Sees a squirt gun. Picks it up and
13 squirts water out of it. He smiles. Gets an idea. He holds
14 the gun to his own back and waves frantically, as if being
15 held up. No attention. He can't believe it. He thinks. He
16 shrugs and goes to throw the squirt gun away. He's face
17 to face with CAL, who thinks he's being held up. He
18 freaks, jumps out of line, and waves for help to the others.
19 No one notices him. NEEDYDUDE shakes his head. It's
20 not a robbery! CAL pulls out his wallet and holds a wad
21 of cash out to NEEDYDUDE, who is shaking his head no.
22 DOE comes by, snatches it, stuffs it into her can. CAL
23 looks at DOE, then at NEEDYDUDE. He squirts CAL with
24 the gun. CAL blusters, smacks NEEDYDUDE over the
25 head with the wallet and falls back into step.
26   NEEDYDUDE rubs his head. He gets into the center
27 of the circle and watches them march by. He has a hunger
28 pang. A bad one. He sits down on the ground, arms
29 wrapped around himself. Shivers. Looks like he's falling
30 asleep. A beat. Falls onto his side, right into the path of
31 the marchers.
32   PREACH stops dead in his tracks. The others crash
33 into him.
34 CAL/DOE: Hey! What's the problem?! Who stopped the line?
35 What're you doing?! I've got to be somewhere! *(A beat)*

1 PREACH: I think he's dead.
2 CAL/DOE: Who? What? What're you talking about?
3 PREACH: *(Pointing down)* Down there. I didn't even see 'im.
4   He was just there. I walked right into 'im.
5 CAL: Too bad.
6 DOE: The poor man. He looks awful. Probably hasn't eaten
7   for days.
8 PREACH: It's freezing out here. I wished I'da seen 'im
9   before.
10 CAL: C'mon! There's a rescue mission across town. Burger
11   King's hiring, right? Get outta the way. I gotta get
12   downtown! *(The drumbeat stops. They look around.)*
13 PREACH/CAL/DOE: Who's there? *(They look up.)* You?! *(They*
14   *point at NEEDYDUDE.)* Him? Well he should have asked
15   for help!
16 PREACH: I've gotta jacket.
17 DOE: *(Shaking can)* I've got a little something in here.
18 CAL: Does he take . . . Mastercard?
19 PREACH/CAL/DOE: *(Looking up)* You? *(Looking down)* Him?
20   *(A beat)* That's not fair! Why didn't you tell us it was you?!
21   *(Blackout)*
22
23
24
25
26
27
28
29
30
31
32
33
34
35

The Right Equipment

*A Sketch on
Using God's Gift*

Max Medina, Brenna Gunn in *The Right Equipment.*

PRODUCTION NOTES

This sketch can be used to illustrate a teaching on using God-given talents and opportunities. It was based on Matthew 25:14-29 and Romans 12:6-8.

CAST: BARRY, HOMELESS LADY, GREASE MONKEY, CHAIN MAN.

SCENE: A city street. The present.

COSTUME NOTE: Modern.

RUNNING TIME: Four to five minutes.

PROPS: Toolbox, can of tuna, quarter, handcuffs, leg irons, garbage can, newspapers.

1   *AT RISE:*   Lights. BARRY runs in carrying a large toolbox.
2

3   **BARRY:** *(Calling after someone)* **Dad! Wait!** *Daaad!* **Hold up,**
4   **will ya?! You spaced your tool — I said** *you forgot your*
5   *toolbox!* *(He stops, trying to catch his breath.)* **No, I said** *you*
6   **forgot it. Whaddaya mean? Wait. Time out. What do I**
7   **want with this thing? No, no, Dad — it's your toolbox.**
8   **Aw, geez, is this one'a those "You're a man now, you need**
9   **your own toolbox" routines? OK, all right, so it's mine**
10   **now. Fine. Great. So how long you gonna be gone? Dad?**
11   *Daaad?* *(Nothing. He sits with a sigh.)*
12   **Aw, man, this is just great. He couldn't pull the old**
13   **"You're a man now, you need your own Jaguar" bit**
14   **instead'a this?** *(Unlatches the toolbox.)* **Whoa. What am I**
15   **doin'? No way. I touch this thing and I'm gonna break**
16   **somethin'. Guaranteed. It's in my genes.** *(Locks it down.)*
17   **Yeah, if something happens to anything before he gets**
18   **back, I'll just tell him I didn't touch a pickin' thing. That's**
19   **my story.** *(He picks up the toolbox and starts off. He passes by*
20   *a HOMELESS LADY. Tries to ignore her.)*
21   **HOMELESS LADY:**   **Hey. Hey, bub. Hey, palsy.**
22   **BARRY:** *(Keeps walking)* **Sorry. No change.**
23   **HOMELESS LADY:**   **Shoot. Wait, hey, wait, will ya?** *(Digs in*
24   *her pocket and pulls out a can of tuna. BARRY is surprised.)*
25   **Ya gotta can opener on ya?**
26   **BARRY:**   **Yeah, sure. In my back pocket.**
27   **HOMELESS LADY:**   **Hey, where'd ya get the toolbox?**
28   **BARRY:**   **My father. What do you care —?**
29   **HOMELESS LADY:**   **Whaddaya got in it?**
30   **BARRY:**   **Just a guess here.** *(Thinks)* **Maybe ... tools?**
31   **HOMELESS LADY:**   **Ain't ya even looked in it?**
32   **BARRY:**   **What's it to ya, lady?** *(Digs out a quarter.)* **Here's a**
33   **quarter, OK?**
34   **HOMELESS LADY:**   **Thanks. Hey, maybe there's a can opener**
35   **in there. Ya never know, hunh? Why'n'cha open'er up?**

1   BARRY: Trust me on this. There's no can opener in here.
2   HOMELESS LADY: Maybe I could just use a screwdriver and
3   a hammer'r somethin', hunh?
4   BARRY: Look, I gave ya a quarter! I'm not opening the
5   toolbox, OK?! *(HOMELESS LADY walks away, mumbling.)*
6   HOMELESS LADY: Why ya carry a thing around ya ain't
7   gonna use? Sheesh!
8   VOICE: *(Off-stage)* Hey, pal! Hey, buddy!
9   BARRY: *(Looking around)* Suddenly I'm everybody's pal.
10   *(BARRY turns and sees GREASE MONKEY in oily overalls*
11   *and a baseball cap.)*
12   GREASE MONKEY: Ya think ya gotta trimensional dual-
13   sided spanner gizmo in that kit a yers there?
14   BARRY: Sorry, Scotty. You can't save the Enterprise this
15   time.
16   GREASE MONKEY: Hey, no really, ya mind if I take a look?
17   It'd help me out big time. *(He moves toward BARRY, who*
18   *backs away, hugging the toolbox.)*
19   BARRY: Get out. You're not looking in my toolbox!
20   GREASE MONKEY: Come on. That's a spiffy kit ya got there.
21   I'm broke down, hunh. One look. That's all it takes.
22   BARRY: I'm not opening my toolbox for anyone, OK? My
23   father gave it to me. It's his, got it? And I'm not gonna
24   use nothin'.
25   GREASE MONKEY: If yer dad *gave* it to ya, then I'm sure he
26   wouldn't mind if ya helped me out —
27   BARRY: He *minds!*
28   GREASE MONKEY: *(Hands up in innocence)* OK, OK! Don't get
29   all squirrelly on me. *(GREASE MONKEY goes out. BARRY*
30   *sighs and turns around. He screams. CHAIN MAN is standing*
31   *there. He has on handcuffs and leg irons.)*
32   CHAIN MAN: Hey, ya think you gotta —?
33   BARRY: *No!*
34   CHAIN MAN: Maybe, like a hacksaw or some —
35   BARRY: *Nothing! Nada! Zippo!*

1 **CHAIN MAN:** *(Gestures at the box.)* **What's that there then?**
2 **BARRY:** *(Backing away)* **A *big* mistake, that's what. Somebody**
3 **just gave this to me, all right? I didn't know I was gonna**
4 **have to like do something with it.**
5 **CHAIN MAN:** **Well, hey, if ya don't want it, I'll take —**
6 **BARRY:** ***No, it's mine!* Now start walking.** *(CHAIN MAN doesn't*
7 *move.)* **Officer!** *Officer!* *(CHAIN MAN splits.)* **This is**
8 **unbelievable. I don't need this kinda grief! I should'a**
9 **never asked Dad for anything. This is the kinda trouble**
10 **I get in.** *(He looks around. Sees a garbage can. Stuffs the toolbox*
11 *in and covers it up with newspapers.)*
12 **That'll work. When he comes back, I'll get his stupid**
13 **toolbox for 'im. He oughta be grateful, anyways. It'll all**
14 **be in one piece when he gets it.** *(Wipes his hands.)* **Yeah,**
15 **he should be real happy I took *noooo* chances with it.**
16 *(BARRY pats the garbage can and goes out, hands stuffed in*
17 *his pockets. Blackout)*
18
19
20
21
22
23
24
25
26
27
28
29
30
31
32
33
34
35

BOUNDARIES AND ADDICTIONS

And the Bulb Goes On

*A Sketch on
Sexual Boundaries*

PRODUCTION NOTES

This sketch was written to be read or acted during a frank discussion or talk on sexual boundaries. It can easily be done as a scene or a Readers Theatre.

The matching word or phrase that ends each line is picked up by the other person, making the dialog a seamless presentation in very different directions.

CAST: RACHEL, GREGG.

SCENE: Two bedrooms. The present.

COSTUME NOTE: Modern, casual.

RUNNING TIME: Four to five minutes.

PROPS: Chairs, table, stuffed animals, CDs.

1 *AT RISE:*   Lights. RACHEL is sitting on a chair, stuffed animals all
2   around her.
3
4 RACHEL: How many guys does it take to screw in a light
5   bulb? *(Pause)* One hundred. One to replace the bulb and
6   ninety-nine to listen to him brag about it. OK, OK. How
7   'bout this? How many nice guys does it take to screw in
8   a light bulb? *(Pause)* Guess we all better get used to
9   reading by candlelight. *(The light picks up GREGG, who is*
10   *sitting on a bench, going through his CDs.)*
11 GREGG: How many girls does it take to screw in a light bulb?
12   *(Pause)* One. But not until she wants to.
13 RACHEL: Look, it's not that I don't like guys. I really like 'em.
14   It's just hard to find one that likes you, you know what
15   I mean? Well, it's easy to find one that'll love you. "Come
16   on, I love you." But the trick is finding one that likes you.
17   You know what like means? Like means they listen to
18   what you want, not just want you and listen later.
19 GREGG: *(Same time)* Later for that. I mean, I got nothing
20   against girls. Hey, some of my best girlfriends've been
21   girls. I just want to find one that realizes I'm only trying
22   to show my love. Gettin' busy is the way you show love
23   in this world. What, you think I'm making this up? Look
24   around you. *(Holds up his CDs.)* It's all right here. It's not
25   an animal kinda thing. I'm just showing my affection.
26 RACHEL: *(Same time)* Affection. That's what I'd really like.
27   But when I've got a hold of one of his hands, and
28   buttoning up my shirt with the other — and wrapping
29   my legs into a figure eight, I don't feel very affectionate
30   anymore. I feel like, "Full power to the shields, Captain,
31   she's going into battle."
32 GREGG: *(Same time)* Battle. Why's it always have to be a
33   battle? It makes me feel like a creep. Like I'm pushing
34   or something. I mean, I get mixed signals. I get all worked
35   up and emotional and all and it's like, "Take me home"

1   and stuff. If she doesn't want my affection, then why does
2   she even kiss me.
3 RACHEL: *(Same time)* Kiss me. That's what I want. Just kiss
4   me. I like it when you kiss me. But if I kiss him, it's the
5   Big Invite. And if I don't kiss him, I'm like a Vulcan or
6   something. Here's the bottom line. This is what I figured
7   out. *(Points to her forehead.)* You know, the bulb finally went
8   on up here. If a guy comes on to you, your boyfriend or
9   a date, and gives you the "it's your fault I'm turned on"
10   routine, you just remember one thing — it is not your
11   responsibility to do something about it.
12 GREGG: *(Same time)* Your responsibility to do something
13   about it. I didn't get this way all by myself. It takes two
14   to tango, remember that. And then when it gets to that
15   point, it's instinct. You can't shut it off.
16 RACHEL: *(Same time)* Can't shut it off? That's a lie, if there
17   ever was one. He can shut it off. And even if he really
18   thinks he can't, that's not your problem. It's his. Let him
19   deal with it. Oh, but you're gonna hear it. You can't get
20   around it. He's gonna say, "You're such a tease."
21 GREGG: *(Same time)* You're such a tease. Girls are teases.
22   That's for total sure. What they wear, the way they kiss
23   you or look at you. What do they expect us to do? How
24   are we supposed to feel? That's what I'm tellin' you. Mixed
25   signals.
26 RACHEL: *(Same time)* Mixed signals?! Don't give mixed
27   signals, then. Just tell the truth. "I like you, I might even
28   be in love with you, but I'm not going to sleep with you
29   or do anything I don't want to do." That's it. Nothing
30   mixed about it. He's not the one who could get pregnant,
31   right? He's not the one giving up something he wants to
32   keep. You are. And if you don't wanna keep it for the one
33   person who deserves it, then all I can say is — you don't
34   know what you're gonna be missing.
35 GREGG: *(Same time)* You don't know what you're gonna be

1   missing. That's what my brother told me when I said I

2   wanted to wait till I got married. I felt like a total geek

3   when he said that. Look, my dad didn't wait. None of my

4   friends are waiting. So, I'm not waiting. And if you are —

5   *(They turn and face each other.)*

6   **GREGG/RACHEL:**   Then don't go out with me.

7   **RACHEL:**   I didn't sign up for the pressure. And anybody who

8   pressures, didn't sign up for me. *(The lights fade to blackout.)*

9

10

11

12

13

14

15

16

17

18

19

20

21

22

23

24

25

26

27

28

29

30

31

32

33

34

35

The Stuff of Life

A Mime on Excess Baggage

L. Enscoe, Lori Thomley in *The Stuff of Life*.

PRODUCTION NOTES

This pantomime was written to be performed in outdoor, camp or large group meetings. It's in broad slapstick style, with room left in for lots of improvisation and original business.

CAST: ZANY ONE, ZANY TWO, ZANY THREE.

SCENE: Entrance to the Kingdom. Timeless.

COSTUME NOTE: Baggy, clown clothes.

RUNNING TIME: Four to five minutes.

PROPS: Wall with hole cut in, signs, duffle bags, horn, binoculars, wagon, trunk, boxes with writing, material possessions — golf clubs, stereo, TV, CDs, etc.

1   *AT RISE:*   A bright wall with a person-size hole cut in the middle
2   halfway up. This is the entrance to the Kingdom. Around the
3   playing area are signs that read: "The Kingdom!" "You Found
4   It!" "Kingdom this Way!"
5
6   **ZANY ONE comes in, dressed like a clown. Two**
7   **bulging duffle bags on his back. One reads "JUST" and**
8   **the other "STUFF." They're very heavy. ZANY ONE is**
9   **looking around with a pair of binoculars. He bumps into**
10   **a sign. He looks up at it with the binoculars. Can't read**
11   **it. Turns the binoculars around. He reads it's the**
12   **Kingdom. He jumps for joy. Claps his hands. Pulls a horn**
13   **out of his pocket and toots it.**
14   **ZANY TWO and THREE rush in, excited and looking**
15   **around.**
16   **ZANY TWO pulls a kid's wagon filled with material**
17   **acquisitions — golf clubs, stereo, TV, etc. A sign on the**
18   **wagon reads, "STUFF I'VE ALWAYS WANTED."**
19   **ZANY THREE has a trunk that reads, "STUFF I'VE**
20   **ALWAYS BELIEVED."**
21   **ZANY ONE honks his horn. The others look over at**
22   **him and see the sign. They point at it, jump for joy, hug**
23   **each other. They look around for the Kingdom. They can't**
24   **find it. They look in the audience — in purses, under hats**
25   **and in bags.**
26   **Meanwhile, ZANY ONE has found the entrance to**
27   **the Kingdom. He looks at the hole. Sticks his head in.**
28   **Looks at the other two and honks his horn.**
29   **ZANY TWO and THREE stop. They see the hole. They**
30   **bolt for it, trying to cram in at the same time. They can't**
31   **fit. They come out. They go at it again. Nothing doing.**
32   **ZANY TWO comes out, points Off-stage. ZANY THREE**
33   **looks. ZANY TWO dives in the hole. ZANY THREE catches**
34   **him and pulls him back.**
35   **ZANY ONE watches this with rolled-eyed boredom.**

1   Finally, ZANY TWO and THREE motion that they
2   should flip for first one in. ZANY THREE points to ZANY
3   ONE's head. ZANY TWO looks at ZANY ONE's backside
4   and grudgingly nods. They flip ZANY ONE over in their
5   arms. ZANY ONE lands, wobbling and woozy. He might
6   fall on his backside or on his head. Finally, he pitches
7   forward onto his head with a honk of his horn.
8   ZANY THREE claps in victory and pushes TWO out
9   of the way for a clear shot at the Kingdom. He jumps in,
10   but his trunk gets stuck. He comes out. He tries several
11   times to get inside with his trunk, but unless he lets go
12   of it — nothing doing. Finally, he sets the trunk down
13   and climbs in solo. He's gone. The other two look at each
14   other in surprise. *Whooosh!* ZANY THREE crashes out of
15   the hole and beelines it for the trunk and hugs it to
16   himself. He kisses it. He can't let go of it. He pushes ZANY
17   TWO to the hole and waves off the Kingdom. He walks
18   out, dejected.
19   ZANY TWO has the same problem. He climbs in, but
20   his wagon won't go. He tries to lift the wagon in. Too
21   much stuff. He comes out and throws a tantrum. ZANY
22   ONE motions that there's too much stuff. Lose some of
23   it. He grabs something to toss. ZANY TWO is all over
24   him, taking his possessions back. ZANY ONE honks and
25   steps aside. Go to it, he's saying.
26   ZANY TWO asks him to help him lift the wagon
27   through. ZANY ONE shakes his head. ZANY TWO
28   implores. ZANY ONE measures the wagon, measures the
29   hole. He shakes his head. It won't fit, doofus, he's saying.
30   He honks for emphasis.
31   ZANY TWO rages. Tries to stuff the wagon through.
32   No go. He slams it down. Looks between the wagon and
33   the Kingdom. Makes for the hole, then turns and dashes
34   to the wagon, hugging the stuff to him. He shakes his
35   head. He's made his choice. He goes out, smugly.

1   ZANY ONE watches him go. He's alone. He honks
2 after them. No response. He waves them off. He goes to
3 the hole and honks. He makes the dive. He won't fit. He
4 sits, dejected. He honks. He has an idea. He pulls off the
5 duffle bags and begins to empty them. They're filled with
6 boxes with writing on them. He takes them out and shows
7 them off.
8   "STUFF I DID THAT I FEEL REAL BAD ABOUT."
9 He throws it into the audience. "STUFF OTHER PEOPLE
10 DID TO ME THAT I FEEL REAL BAD ABOUT." Tosses it.
11 "STUFF I WISH I DID THAT I FEEL REAL BAD ABOUT."
12 Tosses it. "STUFF I WANTED OTHER PEOPLE TO DO
13 THAT I FEEL REAL BAD ABOUT." Tosses it.
14   The bag's empty. He makes another dive. Still won't
15 fit. He empties the second bag like the first. It has the
16 same kind of boxes with writing.
17   "STUFF I THOUGHT WAS IMPORTANT." Throws it
18 into the audience. "STUFF OTHER PEOPLE THOUGHT
19 WAS IMPORTANT." Tosses it. "THE IMPORTANCE OF
20 STUFF." Throws it.
21   He folds the bags and sets them aside. He smiles. He
22 kisses the wall. He takes a deep breath. He honks his
23 horn. He dives into the hole without a hitch. He pops up
24 on the other side. He looks over the wall at the audience.
25 He waves. He honks his horn. He dashes off.
26
27
28
29
30
31
32
33
34
35

The Orca Wimpy Show

A Sketch on
Breaking Addictions

Anne Pirio (L), Heather Morein in *The Orca Wimpy Show.*
(Glendale Presbyterian Church Youth Drama Team)

PRODUCTION NOTES

The Orca Wimpy Show can be used when teaching God's role in breaking addictions, or when discussing Scriptures like Romans 12:2, 1 Corinthians 10:13, 2 Corinthians 3:17, 18, and Philippians 4:13.

CAST: ORCA WIMPY, JIM HAZELNUT, CHERYL NADA, SUSAN GUNNERSMA, MICHAEL CLEANBILL.

SCENE: A TV studio. The present.

COSTUME NOTE: Modern. A set of army fatigues will be needed.

RUNNING TIME: Five to six minutes.

PROPS: Microphone, cue cards, candy wrapper, candy bar, box of chocolates, vegetables.

1   *AT RISE:*   The playing area is unlit.
2
3   ANNOUNCER: *(Off-stage mike)* **And now, live from Warmwater,**
4   **Illinois, please welcome TV's most-loved talk show host —**
5   **Orca Wimpy!** *(Lights. The TECHNICAL DIRECTOR comes*
6   *out carrying the "Applause" sign, encouraging the audience to*
7   *clap. ORCA comes out, mike in hand. She basks in the adulation.)*
8   ORCA: **Thank you. Welcome to the Orca Wimpy Show. How**
9   **many of us are still caught up in behaviors and addictions**
10   **we simply don't want to be a part of our lives anymore?**
11   **Hard question. Just how do we change our lives? How**
12   **do we find relief from these troubling compulsions? Well,**
13   **today we're going to talk to you about how to make those**
14   **changes by tackling one of my favorite topics — food.**
15   **More importantly — chocolate. Any chocolate lovers in**
16   **the audience?** *(Some applause)* **I thought so. Well, today**
17   **we're going to meet some recovering chocoholics to see**
18   **just how they did it. Jim Hazelnut, where are you?** *(JIM*
19   *stands in the audience. He's shaky and nervous, digging through*
20   *his pockets as he speaks.)*
21   JIM: **I'm right here, Orca.** *(ORCA goes to him, mike outstretched.)*
22   **Hi, my name's Jim, and I'm a chocoholic.**
23   ORCA: **Hi, Jim. This chocolate thing. A tough nut to crack.**
24   JIM: **You said it.**
25   ORCA: **Tell us how you did it.**
26   JIM: **Well, Orca. You Sees — see! — I was in real big truffle —**
27   **trouble! I used to sit in my house out in caramel —**
28   **Carmel — just shoveling in the cho . . . cho . . . cho —**
29   ORCA: **Chocolate.**
30   JIM: **Chocolate! I . . . I had to have it, Orca. Night and day.**
31   **Dark, milk, semisweet, bittersweet. It didn't matter.**
32   **When I couldn't get the real thing, I'd eat Baker's cho . . .**
33   **cho . . . cho —**
34   ORCA: **Chocolate.**
35   JIM: **Chocolate! At work my friends would all Snicker —**

1   laugh! — at me when I'd make my daily Mounds —

2   rounds! — with a Baby Ruth in one hand and a Butterfinger

3   in the other. I started developing these Twix — tics! —

4   when I couldn't get cho . . . cho . . . cho . . . the stuff! *(Takes*

5   *a deep breath.)* Then one day, I was at home sitting in a

6   pile of candy wrappers that went up to my navel and I

7   knew it was time to watch my M & Ms — Ps and Qs! So I

8   quit. Just like that. It was a miracle! I don't even crave

9   it! I just said no to cho . . . cho . . . cho —

10 ORCA: Chocolate!

11 JIM: *Chocolate!* I don't need it anymore! Not at all! Uh-uh!

12   No way!

13 ORCA: Incredible story. You did this on your own? Sheer

14   will power?

15 JIM: You bet. I told myself I didn't want it, and now I don't.

16   Hey, I don't care if I ever see the stuff again. Just told

17   my mind that I didn't . . . didn't . . . didn't . . . *(He has found*

18   *an old candy wrapper in a pocket and starts to lick the paper)*

19   . . . want it. Don't want it! Never think about it! *(ORCA*

20   *reaches for the paper.)* **Touch it and die, Wimpy!** *(ORCA pulls*

21   *her hand back. She smiles.)*

22 ORCA: Well. Thank you, Jim, for the inspiration. Let's just

23   talk to Cheryl Nada, shall we? Cheryl? Are you here?

24   Cheryl? *(Someone in the audience is forcing CHERYL to stand*

25   *and shouting, "She's right here!" "She's over here!")*

26 CHERYL: Am not! I am not! No one's calling me — *(CHERYL*

27   *turns and sees ORCA's mike in her face.)* Oh. Ah . . . hi, Orca.

28   How you doing?

29 ORCA: Chocolate. Ruler of your life. Master of your existence.

30   Filled your head night and day.

31 CHERYL: Nuh-uh. I never ate chocolate. Never. Who told you

32   that?

33 ORCA: You did.

34 CHERYL: Oh. OK, so I had a little problem. So kill me.

35 ORCA: You beat the wrapper. Chocoholic no more. Talk.

1 (*CHERYL takes out a Hershey bar and begins to peel the*
2 *wrapper.*)
3 CHERYL: I used to have trouble with chocolate, but not
4   anymore, Orca. I don't even think about chocolate
5   anymore. I never even see chocolate. Completely gone
6   out of my life. Where's chocolate? I don't know!
7 ORCA: (*Staring at the bar*) **Really.**
8 CHERYL: That's right. It's history. (*Holds up the bar.*) Hey,
9   you want some of this banana?
10 ORCA: Maybe just a bit of denial here?
11 CHERYL: Nuh-uh! No way! *Fibber!*
12 ORCA: Sit down, Cheryl. (*CHERYL does.*) Ah, next up is Susan
13   Gunnersma. Susan? (*SUSAN snaps to attention. She's dressed*
14   *in fatigues and has vegetables sticking out of every pocket. She*
15   *snacks on them as she talks.*)
16 SUSAN: Present, sir!
17 ORCA: Susan Gunnersma. Portrait of a Cocoa-Bean Hound.
18   Dish the story.
19 SUSAN: (*PFC delivery*) Met with some chocolate resistance,
20   sir! Assessed the strength of the enemy, sir! Ascertained
21   the need for reinforcements, sir! Enrolled in the
22   Hagelschlag School of Chocolate Warfare in Oak Park,
23   Illinois, sir!
24 ORCA: And how did that help you change your destructive
25   eating patterns?
26 SUSAN: Implemented amended behavior patterns, sir!
27 ORCA: (*D.I. delivery*) I can't heeeaaar yoouuu!
28 SUSAN: *Implemented amended behavior patterns, sir!* Rise
29   at 0500 hours, exercise, eat carrots, oats and tofu eggs.
30   More exercise. Self-help reading period. Lunch: salad,
31   lentil-and-wheat-gluten stew, thirty-seven-grain bread.
32   Laps, KP, and shopping maneuvers. Inspiration period:
33   read "Vegetarian Times," "Self Reliance," and "Your
34   Chakra's Too Small" magazines. Dinner: soy burgers, tofu
35   potatoes, watercress. Lights out, 2100 hours. (*SUSAN*

1   *starts doing jumping jacks.)*
2 ORCA: **Good night! With a schedule like that, there's no**
3   **time to even miss chocolate.**
4 SUSAN: *(Still jumping)* **Sir, yes, sir!**
5 ORCA: **Thank you, Susan. Susan?** *Plant it, soldier!* *(SUSAN*
6   *drops to her seat.)* **All right. We've got will power, denial**
7   **and behavioral modification. Let's get one more opinion.**
8   **Is Michael Cleanbill here?** *(MICHAEL stands, holding a*
9   *pound-box of chocolates.)*
10 MICHAEL: **Here I am, Orca.** *(ORCA sees the chocolates. Tries to*
11   *maintain.)*
12 ORCA: **Well, aren't you brave. A box of cho . . . cho . . . cho —**
13 MICHAEL: **Chocolate.**
14 ORCA: **Chocolate!** *(Regains herself.)* **So, spill the beans.**
15 MICHAEL: **It's been hard, Orca. Really hard. I was way**
16   **overweight and I just kept shoveling down the chocolate.**
17   **It was getting humiliating. I believed with all my heart**
18   **that I couldn't stop eating chocolate. So I started telling**
19   **Jesus about it.**
20 ORCA: **Your therapist?** *(Gets it.)* **Oh, that Jesus! Sorry. Go on.**
21 MICHAEL: **I told Jesus he had more power than I did. Then I**
22   **started talking to a therapist —**
23 ORCA: **Jesus?**
24 MICHAEL: **No, Frank.**
25 ORCA: **OK, sorry. Go on.**
26 MICHAEL: **After a while I began to realize that I ate**
27   **chocolate because I was angry. I wanted someone — or**
28   **something — to care about me. To love me. But this box**
29   **of chocolates didn't love me. I had to let God love me.**
30   **Then I could start loving myself. After a while, I just**
31   **started losing interest in cramming it in my face.**
32 ORCA: **That easy?**
33 MICHAEL: **Easy? No. Definitely not easy. But lasting.**
34   *(MICHAEL takes a chocolate out and nibbles it. ORCA watches,*
35   *panting.)* **Hey, wanna chocolate, Orca?**

1   ORCA: No thanks, I'm on a diet. Oh, I forgot!
2   MICHAEL: What's that?
3   ORCA: I said I'd never diet again! *(She drops her face into the*
4   *chocolate box and starts chewing. MICHAEL watches a moment,*
5   *then takes the mike.)*
6   MICHAEL: Well, it looks like that's it for Orca Wimpy today.
7   Watch tomorrow when she'll be talking about — *(ORCA*
8   *mumbles something with a mouthful.)* Jelly-filled and coffee,
9   the new way to reach that target heart rate! Good night,
10   everyone! *(ORCA looks up. She gives the "cut it" sign.*
11   *Blackout.)*
12
13
14
15
16
17
18
19
20
21
22
23
24
25
26
27
28
29
30
31
32
33
34
35

The Late Great Teen Museum

*A Sketch on
Surviving the Teen Years*

PRODUCTION NOTES

This sketch was written for a more ambitious group. It can involve the entire youth group as at least fifteen actors are needed.

The TEENS are played by the same six actors. The GROUP can be played by as many youth group members as desired.

Your mission, should you decide to accept it . . .

CAST: MS. GYDE, VOICE, GROUP (ten or more), TEENS (at least six), BRIGHT KID.

SCENE: A futuristic natural history museum.

COSTUME NOTE: Futuristic and present day.

RUNNING TIME: Twelve to fifteen minutes.

PROPS: Booklets, remote, beer cans, liquor bottle, TV, telephone, magazine, benches, mall sign, fast food, name shopping bags, Walkmans.

1   *AT RISE:*   The playing area is dark. MS. GYDE is standing at the
2   top of the aisle, gazing up into the darkness, lost in thought. A
3   voice on an intercom system can be heard.
4
5   VOICE: *(On mike)* **Ms. Gyde.** *(Pause)* **Excuse me, Ms. Gyde?**
6   GYDE: *(Coming to)* **Oh, sorry. Yes, I'm right here.**
7   VOICE: *(On mike)* **The afternoon tour has just beamed down.**
8   **They're in the transporter room. Are you ready for them**
9   **now?**
10 GYDE: **Yes, I am. Send them in please.** *(Doors open in back.*
11   *Laughter and talking. A GROUP of high school kids come up*
12   *the aisles carrying booklets. All are dressed in futuristic clothes.)*
13   **Good afternoon, students. I'm Ms. Gyde . . .** *(Nobody*
14   *is listening)* **. . . excuse me . . . class? Ah, I'd like to welcome**
15   **you all to . . .** *(No one is paying attention. MS. GYDE pulls out*
16   *a remote, points it at the kids and squeezes. They immediately*
17   *shut up and spin around to face her, the perfect, attentive*
18   *audience.)*
19   **I could just kiss the guy that invented this puppy.**
20   **Good afternoon, class. I'd like to welcome you all to "The**
21   **Late Great Teen Museum."** *(She remotes the playing area. A*
22   *section lights up. A strange sight. What is revealed is something*
23   *like a natural history museum display. Six TEENS are frozen*
24   *in position dressed like the nineties. They are smiling and waving*
25   *at each other. The GROUP oohs and ahhs at the sight. MS.*
26   *GYDE remotes off the light.)*
27   **Doesn't that look wonderful?** *(The GROUP nods and*
28   *talks to each other.)* **Let's start with introductions, shall**
29   **we? I'm Ms. Gyde. I'm your tour leader here at the "Late**
30   **Great Teen Museum," which was established in 2090 to**
31   **give today's teens a chance to see what it must have been**
32   **like to be a teenager in the late twentieth century —**
33   **roughly one hundred years ago — just before their near**
34   **extinction. So, any questions so far?** *(Nothing)* **Well, good.**
35   **I'll start with one. How are all of you this afternoon?**

1   **GROUP:**   **Way live! Awesome! Radical! Dudical!**

2   **GYDE:** *(Delighted)* **Wonderful! I see you've all read your**
3   **booklets on ancient teen slang. You almost had me**
4   **convinced ... dudes!** *(The GROUP laughs.)* **Well, good.**
5   **Let's move on to our first exhibit, shall we?** *(They walk to*
6   *the playing area.)* **Please stay behind the red lines. If**
7   **anyone has a personal force field switched on, a Sony**
8   **nuclear stereo aural implant, or a Kodak mini-hologram**
9   **pupil cam corder going, please turn them off, as they are**
10   **not allowed in the museum.** *(Several of the GROUP stop to*
11   *push buttons on themselves.)*

12   **Fine. Now, we're about to go into the dark ages, kids.**
13   **A time when teenagers used things like video tape,**
14   **compact discs and listened to music called metal, pop,**
15   **rap and reggae. And here we are at our first exhibit.** *(She*
16   *remotes the lights on in an exhibit. The TEENS are partying.*
17   *Frozen in motion.)*

18   **Group, this is what was known as "partying."**
19   **Getting wasted was another way these teenagers spoke**
20   **about this harmless recreational activity meant to relieve**
21   **tension, build lasting relationships with others and**
22   **fantasize about how one's problems were ... a major**
23   **drag, and worse than anyone else's problems.** *(A hand goes*
24   *up in the GROUP.)* **Yes, I see that hand.**

25   **BRIGHT KID:**   **If partying was harmless, how come those**
26   **guys almost went extinct?**

27   **GYDE:**   **My, what an interesting question. Any others?**
28   *(Nothing)* **No? Good, let's move on. Since these exhibits**
29   **are made up of live-action cybernetic organisms, we can**
30   **listen in on what a ... party must have been like.** *(She*
31   *pushes the remote. Top forty music starts playing. The partying*
32   *TEENS come to life, drinking beer, smoking dope, passing a*
33   *bottle around. It's all lighthearted, laughing and friendly.)*

34   **As you can see, it was a happy time in the lives of**
35   **these young people. A time to ... cut loose, as they said.**

1   To enjoy life. To let drugs and alcohol enhance life. To

2   let substances . . . intensify the personality.

3   BRIGHT KID: What if you're a jerk to begin with?

4   GYDE: Yes . . . an intriguing thought. You're so full of . . .

5   interesting thoughts, aren't you? *(Something is going wrong*

6   *with the exhibit. The music screeches to a halt. One of the TEENS*

7   *suddenly collapses to the ground.)*

8   GROUP TEEN: Hey, what's going on up there?

9   GYDE: *(Frantically pushing the remote)* **Something's . . . wrong.**

10   It's supposed to stop.

11   BEER DRINKER: *(In exhibit)* **Dudes! Mark passed out, man.**

12   *(Kneels next to passed-out teen.)* **Hey, Mark. Mark! Quit jokin'**

13   **around, man. Knock it off! You guys, he's not movin'!**

14   *(People shout, "He's wasted!" "Let 'im sleep!")*

15   I told you not to do dust, man. I told you. You're

16   such an idiot! *(Pushing him)* **Jerk! Jerk! I told you!**

17   GYDE: *(Squeezing the remote)* **Don't listen to this! It's not in the**

18   program. Just don't pay any attention.

19   BRIGHT KID: I don't know, looks like a good time to me.

20   *(One of the TEENS in the exhibit comes Downstage, holding a*

21   *bottle of liquor.)*

22   LIQUOR DRINKER: I swear, all I'm askin' is for someone to

23   notice me, man. That's all. I mean, you can mess me over,

24   y'know. But don't ignore me. Am I supposed to feel like

25   this? How am I supposed to feel? Who's supposed to listen

26   to me? Who's supposed to hear me? Don't ignore me. God,

27   if you really love me, don't ignore me, man. If you're

28   listening, please — *(The partying TEENS freeze. MS. GYDE*

29   *has shut the exhibit down with the remote. The lights go out.)*

30   GYDE: *(Very relieved)* **Whew, that did it. I'm sure I have no idea**

31   what all the talk was about. Somebody must have done

32   some reprogramming. Well, anyway, let's move on to the next

33   exhibit, shall we? We're going to take another look at some

34   tension-release recreational behavior. *(She remotes on an*

35   *exhibit. Two VIDEO GUYS are watching videos. PHONE DUDE*

1   *is listening on the phone. MAG MAN is looking at a magazine.*
2   *LOVER BOY and LOVER GIRL are Downstage, snuggling.)*
3   **These teens are involved in various harmless sexual**
4   **activities that were readily available to them at the time.**
5   **Let me see, there's the pornographic video, the sex phone**
6   **line, the skin magazines, and of course, actual bodily contact.**
7   **GROUP TEEN:**   **Wow. Where'd they get all that stuff? Their**
8   **parents?**
9   **GYDE:**   **No. They didn't need their parents to get all this**
10   **"stuff," as you say. For a couple of what they called dollars**
11   **you could get as much of it as you wanted at a, what do**
12   **you call it? Oh yes, a convenience store. Let's listen in,**
13   **hmmm?** *(She remotes the scene to life. Music. The TEENS are*
14   *enjoying themselves.)*
15   **VIDEO GUYS:**   **A couple'a tapes a week! That's all we ask!**
16   **Dude, I swear. I watch this stuff and it gets me ready for**
17   **the weekend. Babes, watch out! We're on nuclear**
18   **detonation! We're gonna get what we want! Babes, all we**
19   **gotta say is —** *Just don't say no!*
20   **PHONE DUDE:**   **Hey, this one's great. It's the pizza man one!**
21   *(To himself)* **Man, where am I gonna get the money to pay**
22   **for all these calls?**
23   **GYDE:**   **Oh, no.**
24   **MAG MAN:**   **Oh, maaaan! Phenomenal.** *(Closes his eyes.)* **I can**
25   **see myself in there, man. I love these photos, man. They**
26   **stay in my head forever.**
27   **LOVER GIRL:**   **You think this is funny?! You get what I'm**
28   **tellin' you? I'm pregnant! You got that in your stupid**
29   **head!**
30   **GYDE:**   Not again. *(Pushes the button.)* **What is going on today?**
31   **LOVER BOY:**   **You weren't protecting yourself?**
32   **LOVER GIRL:**   **You never even asked me if I was!**
33   **LOVER BOY:**   **It's all your fault.** *Your fault!*
34   **LOVER GIRL:**   **Who else you been with? Who? Tell me! Am I**
35

1   gonna have to get a test? Hunh? *Am I gonna have to get*
2   *an AIDS test? (The exhibit freezes. The lights go off.)*
3 GYDE: Well, I'm very sorry, kids. You weren't supposed to see
4   any of that. I just don't know what's up with these
5   teenagers.
6 BRIGHT KID: Well, if you don't know, who does? *(MS. GYDE*
7   *and BRIGHT KID lock eyes for a minute. The GROUP stares*
8   *at MS. GYDE for an answer.)*
9 GYDE: Yes, well, I think we should probably move on,
10   hmmm? There's just one more exhibit before we move
11   into the hands-on room where you can actually touch a
12   CD, listen to a Walkman, and have a taste of Twinkies
13   we discovered in an archeological dig a few years ago.
14   Can you believe they were still fresh? *(She remotes on the*
15   *next display. It's a mall. Several benches and a sign listing the*
16   *mall hours. MALL TEENS are frozen in position listening to*
17   *Walkmans, carrying shopping bags, sodas, fast food.)*
18   Isn't this wonderful? The teenagers of one hundred
19   years ago used to gather at social centers known as "The
20   Mall." Here they greeted one another, ate and drank junk
21   food and listened to portable music machines called
22   Walkmans. Let's take a look-see. Everyone cross your
23   fingers and see if this works. *(GYDE pushes the remote.*
24   *Lights and music. The MALL TEENS start greeting each other*
25   *with high-fives, handshakes, and hugs. It's the picture of good*
26   *times. Then it happens. The kids suddenly stop and face forward*
27   *with dead looks on their faces. The music squeals to a halt. MS.*
28   *GYDE wildly pushes the remote.)* Not again! You're supposed
29   to be having fun! You're supposed to be happy! *(The MALL*
30   *TEENS speak their lines quickly.)*
31 MALL TEEN 1:   Man, I don't believe it. I must'a spent every
32   minute'a my summer in this stinkin' place.
33 MALL TEEN 2:   Hanging around with people I don't even
34   know. Don't even like.
35 MALL TEEN 3:   Who cares? Nobody even knows I'm here.

1   Nobody even cares.

2   MALL TEEN 4: I dunno ... I feel safe here. Nobody knows
3   me. I can melt in and just be forgotten.

4   GYDE: *(Waving remote)* **Stop it! Laugh, talk, smile! You're too**
5   **young to be depressed!**

6   MALL TEEN 5: The same faces every day. Man, we can't all
7   keep comin' here forever.

8   MALL TEEN 6: I wish this place was open all night. Then I
9   wouldn't hafta go home.

10   MALL TEEN 2: I once bought something in every store of the
11   mall one Saturday. Only thing I did I was ever proud of.

12   MALL TEEN 4: Sometimes I don't even have the energy to
13   come down here. I just lay in my room all by myself. Who
14   cares, anyway. *(BRIGHT KID jumps into the exhibit. The*
15   *MALL TEENS all turn and stare at him, amazed.)*

16   GYDE: You get back here, young man! Get out of that display.
17   Those are very delicate machines. Don't touch any of them!
18   Don't you move them!

19   BRIGHT KID: You're machines, right? *(The MALL TEENS*
20   *nod.)* That the way you feel? Nothing alive inside? Nothing
21   feels alive? *(They nod again.)* Look at me. I've got real skin
22   on and I've felt that way! A lot of us have. Any of you know
23   who created you? *(They shake their heads.)*

24   GYDE: I don't like where this is going! Not one bit. *(Into*
25   *remote)* Security! Exhibit area three!

26   BRIGHT KID: If I told you who made you, would that make a
27   difference to you? *(They nod their heads.)*

28   MALL TEEN 1: I could ask him why he made me.

29   MALL TEEN 2: I could ask him what I'm doing here. *(The*
30   *GROUP moves into the exhibit, touching the MALL TEENS in*
31   *amazement.)*

32   MALL TEEN 3: I could ask him if he remembers me.

33   MALL TEEN 4: I could tell him I wasn't happy.

34   MALL TEEN 5: I could ask him if he knew where I was going.

35   MALL TEEN 6: I could tell him I was afraid.

1   MALL TEEN 4:   I could ask him to put life inside me.

2   MALL TEEN 1:   I could . . . ask him to put life inside me.

3   GYDE: This tour has officially concluded.

4   BRIGHT KID: I've got something I want to tell them! *(MS.*

5   *GYDE aims the remote and squeezes. The MALL TEENS go*

6   *back to their original positions and freeze.)*

7   GYDE: I want all of you to come out of there. Right now. *(The*

8   *GROUP comes out of the exhibit. BRIGHT KID hangs back to*

9   *a moment, then comes out and joins them.)* **This exhibit is**

10   **closed for repairs. You will all beam up to your school**

11   **satellite bus immediately. This field trip is now over.** *(MS.*

12   *GYDE stalks down the aisle. The GROUP does not move. They*

13   *continue to stare at the exhibit.)* **I said come along! What is**

14   **wrong with teens today?** *(She goes out, shouting into her*

15   *remote.)* **Security! Security! Group of questioning**

16   **teenagers in exhibit area three!** *(Small pause. The GROUP*

17   *turns to BRIGHT KID.)*

18   GROUP TEEN: You got something to say, say it. *(Blackout)*

19

20

21

22

23

24

25

26

27

28

29

30

31

32

33

34

35

Over the Fence

A Sketch on
God's Boundaries

PRODUCTION NOTES

Over the Fence is a sketch on God's boundaries and the fall of humanity. You might want to use it during a study of Genesis 3:1-24, Romans 3:23 or 5:12-17 or with a discussion or sermon on God's infinite care for us and his boundaries of life and death.

A, E and BULLY can either be played by children or teens dressed up and playing children.

CAST: A, a little boy; E, a little girl; MR. TAKECARE, a man; BULLY, an older kid.

SCENE: A playground. The present.

RUNNING TIME: Five minutes.

COSTUME NOTE: Bright, modern.

PROPS: Boxes, crates, a seesaw, A-frame ladders, a big ladder.

1   *AT RISE:*   The playing area is covered with different sized acting
2   blocks and crates in primary colors. There is a seesaw and
3   several A-frame ladders. One big ladder stands above the rest.
4   A and E enter. They wander around in awe and excitement.
5
6   A: **Wow. This park is really neat!**
7   E: **Yeah. Look at all this cool stuff to jump on and stuff.** *(They*
8   *run around and look at everything. They come to the big ladder.)*
9   **Wow, that's really way up. Really scary, huh? We could**
10   **really fall a long way.**
11 A: **Yeah. Hey, I betcha we could see everything from up there.**
12   **All around to everything.** *(A laughs and climbs up one of the*
13   *small ladders.)* **High up! Look how high up I am! Really,**
14   **really high up! Can touch the sky almost!**
15 E: **Don't fall down, goofy head!** *(A climbs down. They climb all*
16   *over, challenging each other. "Hey, I can balance!" "Hey, I got*
17   *my eyes closed!" "Hey, I'm higher!" etc.)*
18 A: **Look! I'm the most topperest!** *(Looks out toward the audience.)*
19   **Wow. I can see the big fence from here. Way, way, way**
20   **over there.**
21 E: **Wonder what's on the other side? Do you wonder?** *(MR.*
22   *TAKECARE comes in, dressed in overalls, and a cap. A red rag*
23   *hangs out of his back pocket.)*
24 MR. TAKECARE: **Hey! You havin' fun in here?**
25 A & E: **Sure are, Mr. Takecare!**
26 MR. TAKECARE: *(To A)* **Now you be careful up there. Climb**
27   **all the way up, if you want, but don't stand on the top of**
28   **it, OK? You might — aw, you'll be all right.** *(Walks around*
29   *the playing area.)* **Climb on anything you want. Explore all**
30   **around the place.** *(Stops at the big ladder.)* **Listen, there's**
31   **something I want to tell both of you. I don't want you to**
32   **climb on this one, hear me? It's way too tall. It's**
33   **dangerous. I don't want you to get hurt. That's my rule,**
34   **OK? Climb on it and you'll be sorry. That's all I have to**
35   **say about it. You both understand?** *(A & E nod.)* **Good.**

1   That's very good. *(Looks around.)* **I think you're going to**
2   **like this place. You guys holler if you need me.** *(MR.*
3   *TAKECARE goes out. A & E play around as before. They end*
4   *up near the big ladder. Hesitantly, they touch it. They look*
5   *around, flinching. Nothing happens. They both touch it some*
6   *more. Nothing. They get bored with it.)*
7 A: **Forget that! Let's play on the seesaw!**
8 E: **Yeah!** *(They jump on the seesaw and start pumping. They crane*
9   *their necks to look over to the big fence.)*
10 A: **See anything? Can you see —**
11 E: **Saw the fence!**
12 A: **Can you see Mr. Takecare?**
13 E: **Nuh-uh. Can't see him. Wonder where he is?** *(BULLY comes*
14   *out from behind a crate. He quietly sneaks over to the big ladder*
15   *and leans against it. A & E don't see him.)*
16 A: *(To E)* **Hey, you think Mr. Takecare's gone?**
17 BULLY: **A'course he's gone, ya goofballs! He's long gone! He's**
18   **history!** *(A & E start with surprise.)* **Aw, he just yells at ya**
19   **then he takes off. He always does that.**
20 A: **Gee, who are you?**
21 BULLY: *(Mimicking)* **Gee, who am I? I'm yer pal, that's who,**
22   **stupid head! I know this place. I know all about it, ya**
23   **see. I can show ya around — if ya want me to. I can fill**
24   **ya in on everything. But first ya both need to get a good**
25   **look around. So, why'ncha climb this ladder here and**
26   **take a peek?** *(A gets off the seesaw. E crashes to the ground.)*
27 A: **Hey, Mr. Takecare told us to stay away from that!**
28 BULLY: **Aw c'mon, lamebrain! Mr. Takecare just don't**
29   **wancha seein' over the fence, that's all. But that's exactly**
30   **what'cha wanna do, right? Am I right?** *(A & E nod their*
31   *heads.)* **Lissee here. If you guys see over the fence, then**
32   **you'll know as much about this place as he does. And he**
33   *haaaates* **that! He wants to be Mr. Bigpants, get it? Come**
34   **on, ya scaredy cats! All the rest'a us know what's over**
35   **the fence! Ya wanna grow up smart, doncha? Ya don't**

1   **wanna be stupid all yer life, do ya? Go ahead. He ain't**
2   **around, anyways. Climb on up.**
3   E: **I don't think we oughta.**
4   BULLY: **I dare ya! I double dare ya!** *(A & E look at each other.)*
5   **I quadruple eleventy times double dare ya!** *(That does it.*
6   *A & E dash to the big ladder and climb up opposite sides. BULLY*
7   *beelines it Off-stage.)*
8   A: **You see sumthin'?**
9   E: **Nun-uh. Just the fence!** *(To BULLY)* **Hey, ya big**
10   **fibberhead! You said we could see . . . hey, where'd ya go?**
11   **Where'd he go?**
12   A: **Dunno! Geddown fast! We're in big trouble!** *(They start down*
13   *the big ladder. They see MR. TAKECARE standing there. They*
14   *freeze.)*
15   MR. TAKECARE: *(Sadly)* **Come on down from there.** *(A & E*
16   *climb down, slowly. Heads hung low.)*
17   E: **We're really sorry, Mr. Takecare.**
18   A: **Yeah, this kid came in here and told us to —**
19   MR. TAKECARE: **Shhhh.** *(They watch as MR. TAKECARE*
20   *stacks the blocks and ladders to the side. All except the big*
21   *ladder.)*
22   A: **What'cha doin'?**
23   E: **Where we goin'?**
24   MR. TAKECARE: **Over the fence. The park is closed. Come**
25   **on.** *(He goes out. A & E start to cry.)*
26   A: **No! We don't wanna go! Wait up! Mr. Takecare! We wanna**
27   **stay here! Mr. Takecare, we wanna stay here!** *(Small pause)*
28   E: **He's not gonna let us stay here, is he?** *(Pause)* **We're never**
29   **gonna get back in, are we?**
30   A: **But I don't wanna go over the fence. I'm . . . a'scared. I**
31   **never been a'scared before. I'm a'scared to go over the**
32   **fence!** *(They both look off toward the fence.)* **I don't think**
33   **there's a playground out there.**
34   E: **Hey. You think he'll take care of us out there, too?** *(They*
35   *hold hands and go off. The lights fade to blackout.)*

HOLIDAYS

Get With the Program

A Monolog for
Kick-Off Night

PRODUCTION NOTES

This sketch was written to be used for the Homecoming or kick-off youth group meeting in September. It can be used to illustrate a talk on both the fellowship and more spiritually serious nature of meeting together.

If you want to use it later in the year, some careful editing can be done to preserve the message of the sketch and remove the "welcome back to church" material.

CAST: JESSICA, a high school student.

SCENE: A youth group room. The present.

COSTUME NOTE: Modern.

RUNNING TIME: Four to five minutes.

PROPS: File folders, computer paper, flyers, sign-up sheets.

1   *AT RISE:*   Lights. JESSICA stands there with an armful of file
2   folders, flyers, handouts, etc.
3
4   JESSICA: **Hi, everybody. It is like so totally great to see all**
5   **of you after the whole summer! Welcome back to church!**
6   **Some of you like haven't been here for a while.** *(Searching*
7   *the audience)* **Lauren, Rachel, Tim, Jim, Michael. I see you**
8   **guys! And where've you guys been all summer? First**
9   **Church of the Mall?!** *(She laughs. Sees someone.)*
10   **Hi, Tiffany! How you doin'? No, like I haven't talked**
11   **to you or anything for like two months because you never**
12   **called and my name's in the phone book so don't try that**
13   **one. So, how're you and Mark?! Oh, I'm totally sorry. No,**
14   **I totally didn't know Mark was a scum-sucking**
15   **dweebhead. Does that mean you like cut 'im loose and**
16   **stuff? Really? He's a roamer dude? I . . . I wanna talk to**
17   **you later, OK? Anyway, hi, I'm Jessica. I'm the program**
18   **coordinator for youth group this year. Just like I was**
19   **last year. And the year before, but anyway, since this is**
20   **Kickoff Youth Group Night for the new year here at**
21   **church, I just wanted to let you know about some of the**
22   **programs and stuff we're gonna do so you can keep 'em**
23   **in mind, OK? Get out your Day Runners. There'll be a**
24   **quiz, OK. Just kidding. Has anyone here like gotten**
25   **homework yet? First day, Mrs. Lonnigan, geometry. I**
26   **couldn't believe it. Anyway, programs.** *(Unfolds a huge*
27   *computer list that drapes to the floor.)*
28   **Remember, in two weeks we're going to have our**
29   **all-night volleyball tournament with the junior highers**
30   **and in three weeks we're going to Splashdown Scream**
31   **City Waterslide and Theme Park for some awesome**
32   **fellowship.**
33   **Also, this month we're going to have two ice cream**
34   **fellowships and three Christian Music Nights at the**
35   **skating rink. In October there's four fall get-togethers,**

1 two harvest festivals and we're putting on a haunted
2 house for the little kids. Not too scary, OK? Frank, the
3 Freddie Krueger costume is out. Come dressed like leaves
4 or pumpkins or Moses or something.
5   In December, we're going to go caroling three times
6 and we're going to have a Christmas tree lot fund raiser.
7 Remember the Christmas cantata, the pageant, and the
8 youth group Christmas party! You're going to need to
9 bring stuff. I'm not baking everything again, OK?
10   In January, there's the New Year's party, broom ball,
11 three Christian nights at the skating rink, pressing on
12 to the Higher Goalie Christian hockey night and our snow
13 shoveling party. February is our ski trip, four family film
14 nights, our Winter Volleyball Tournament, and our
15 Valentine Bake-off fund raiser and dinner. Sherry, isn't
16 that where you and Rick met, you little lovebirds? Oh,
17 he's with Carla now. Sorry, Carla. Sorry, Sherry.
18   Well, in March it's Get-Ready-for-Spring fellowship
19 and fashion show, two Christian skating nights, a Hot
20 Fudge Sundae social and our Spring Cleaning fund
21 raiser. In April, it's our Spring Break week at Mt.
22 Golgotha Christian Camp, the Easter cantata, and we're
23 serving for the big all-church Easter brunch. Some'a you
24 guys better show up this year.
25   In May we have Christian concert night, two
26 Christian roller skate nights, School's-Almost-Out bake
27 fund raiser, two car washes and our annual tour to
28 Christian colleges. Then in June — mark this on your
29 calendars — in June we have the big Pancake Breakfast
30 fund raiser. We need you all here for that. There's a
31 School's Out party, a beach trip, a weekend at Camp
32 Golgotha, and finally, a trip to Splashdown Scream City
33 Waterslide for Christian Rock Me on the Water night!
34 *(She laughs and pulls out flyers and forms.)*
35   OK, I've got flyers and sign-up sheets for

1 everything! I had my dad make all these up on the
2 MacIntosh! Full color and stuff! OK, I'm going to pass
3 these around. And sign up for the fund raisers, you guys!
4 Or else how are we gonna pay for all the fun stuff? OK,
5 Travis and Sally, would you help me pass these around?
6 *(Starts to hand out the flyers and looks up.)*
7   What did you say, Andrea? Bible study? Well, I . . .
8 *(She looks on her computer list)* . . . well, I could swear I
9 scheduled in some time for . . . *(Looks up.)* Huh? Prayer
10 time? *(Looks at the list.)* Well, I don't think . . . I . . . I guess
11 not. Well, there must've been a good reason I didn't
12 schedule them in! Look, we just don't have enough time
13 for everything, OK? Don't you think we're busy enough
14 as it is without adding in more time for all that . . . stuff?
15 Look . . . look, Andrea, I don't know why you're so upset.
16 Andrea, this is a youth group, OK? If you wanna pray
17 and read the Bible do it on your own time! *(Pause. She
18 smiles.)* OK, now that we got that settled, who wants to
19 volunteer to bring donuts next week? *(Blackout.)*
20
21
22
23
24
25
26
27
28
29
30
31
32
33
34
35

Nothing Scares Mark Butler

A Sketch for Halloween

PRODUCTION NOTES

This sketch is intended for a Halloween party or special alternative church program. It can be used in conjunction with a discussion or talk on behaviors and beliefs that lead to spiritual death — and sometimes physical death.

CAST: VOICE, MARK BUTLER, VANESSA, JASON, THE SAT TEACHER, CARL, JULIE, DAD'S VOICE, JOEY, A ZOMBIE.

SCENE: Various locations. The present.

COSTUME NOTE: Modern. A zombie outfit.

RUNNING TIME: Ten minutes.

PROPS: Books, Walkman, hockey mask, tests, pencils, Nestle's Quik, Cap'n Crunch, stuffed animals, bench, pillow, paper bag, video.

1   *AT RISE:*   In the darkness we hear scary music. Maybe scary
2   sounds from a Halloween sound effects tape. It should be fairly
3   corny.
4
5   **VOICE:** *(Off-stage)* **Nothing scares Mark Butler.** *(Lights.*
6   *MARK BUTLER comes in, major cool, carrying books and*
7   *tripping to his Walkman.)* **He's not scared of Jason.** *(JASON*
8   *in his hockey mask appears, screaming and grabbing at MARK.*
9   *MARK gives him a look, pushes him aside and keeps walking.)*
10   **He's not scared of the SAT test.** *(TEACHER comes in holding*
11   *a stack of tests and a huge fistful of No. 2 pencils. She's dressed*
12   *like a frump and cackles evilly, coming at MARK.)*
13   **TEACHER:**   **No talking! No drinking! No eating! Fill in the**
14   **bubble completely! You have thirty seconds to finish the**
15   **test!** *(MARK looks her over. Takes a test. Tears it in half and*
16   *flings it. Laughs and keeps walking.)*
17   **VOICE:** *(Off-stage)* **He's not even scared of his little sister**
18   **Vanessa.** *(VANESSA, a creepy junior higher comes in, holding*
19   *squeezable Nestle's Quik, a box of Cap'n Crunch with*
20   *Crunchberries, and stuffed animals.)*
21   **VANESSA:** *(Ranting)* **You're sucha dork! I'm tellin' Mom!**
22   ***Moooom!* No way! Nuh-uh! No-duh! Mom, he's drinking**
23   **out of the milk bottle! Mom, Mark won't let me watch**
24   **Muppet Babies! Mom, Mark's buggin' me!** *(MARK pulls off*
25   *his earphones and looks at us. He gets the willies.)*
26   **VOICE:** *(Off-stage)* **OK, maybe he was scared for a second. But**
27   **then he got over it.** *(MARK pushes VANESSA aside.)*
28   **VANESSA:**   *I'm tellin'! Mooom!* *(She runs off. MARK puts his*
29   *earphones on and keeps walking.)*
30   **VOICE:** *(Off-stage)* **No, Mark Butler wasn't scared of**
31   **anything.** *(A clap of thunder)* **Until he saw his own life.**
32   *(Blackout)*
33   **MARK:**   Hey, what's going on? Hey, what is this?!
34   **VOICE:** *(Off-stage)* **That's when Mark got really, really scared.**
35   *(Lights up. MARK is sitting on a bench. CARL is sitting on the*

1   *ground. They're laughing.)*

2   **CARL:**   **You're doggin' me!**

3   **MARK:**   **She was incredible! I'm tellin' you!**

4   **CARL:**   **I never thought she'd do that. I'm amazed.**

5   **MARK:**   **The right buttons, dude. That's all you gotta know.**

6   **Besides, it was bound to happen. We love each other.**

7   **CARL:**   **Does anybody else in youth group know . . . about**

8   **last night?**

9   **MARK:**   **Just you . . . and Snarfy. But he'll keep his mouth**

10 **shut.** *(JULIE walks in. She's furious. They see her.)*

11 **CARL:**   *(Bolting)* **Dude, I gotta get into the service!** *(JULIE stands*

12 *there with her hands folded, steaming. MARK looks pretty*

13 *scared.)*

14 **MARK:**   **Hi, Julie.**

15 **JULIE:**   **I hope you're proud of yourself.**

16 **MARK:**   **W-what did I do?**

17 **JULIE:**   **It's hard enough fighting you off every weekend,**

18 **now I gotta fight off your lies?**

19 **MARK:**   **Julie, it's about time, man! We've been dating for**

20 **two months!**

21 **JULIE:**   **That's two months too long.** *(She walks out. MARK*

22 *looks at the audience. Blackout.)*

23 **VOICE:**   **Ooooo, now that's a nightmare! Let's hope Mark**

24 **wakes up soon! Well, what do you know? Looks like he's**

25 **just about to.** *(Lights up. MARK is lying on a pillow on the*

26 *bench. He wakes up. He's hung over. Big time. There's a large*

27 *paper bag by his "bed.")*

28 **MARK:**   *Who blew up my head!* *(He winces. Looks in the paper bag.*

29 *Realizes what's inside.)* **Oh, no. What happened? What did**

30 **I do? I told my dad I wouldn't drink. I'm such an idiot!**

31 **Man, I feel so gross. This is supposed to be fun? Frank**

32 **told me drinking vermouth, beer, Jack Daniels and**

33 **Bacardi was supposed to be fun! God, I wish somebody**

34 **would just bury me. Lassie! Lassie boy! Come and bury**

35 **me!** *(A knock at the door)*

1   **DAD'S VOICE:**   Mark?

2   **MARK:**   *(Sitting up)* **Dad!**

3   **DAD'S VOICE:**   **I want to talk to you about the car.** *(Scary*

4   *music. MARK looks at the audience in terror. Blackout.)*

5   **VOICE:**   **Ooooo, scary, kids! This story is getting really scary!**

6   **Look around every corner! Keep your eyes open! Listen**

7   **for the sound of footsteps creeping up behind you . . .** *(The*

8   *sound of footsteps in the darkness)* **Getting closer . . . closer**

9   **. . . closer . . .** ***Look out!*** *(Lights up. JOEY comes up behind*

10   *MARK and grabs his shoulder.)*

11   **MARK:**   *(Spinning around)* ***Ahhh!***

12   **JOEY:**   **A little tense? Too much hot chocolate?**

13   **MARK:**   **Don't do that, Joey!**

14   **JOEY:**   **Why're you so freaked out?** *(He holds up a video.)* **It was**

15   **a piece of cake. They don't ask your age or nothin'. No**

16   **ID. It's not like buying beer, doofus. It's just a harmless**

17   **porno tape.**

18   **MARK:**   **Fine, fine. Let's get outta here.**

19   **JOEY:**   **'Fraid somebody from church might see us?**

20   **MARK:**   **Aren't you?**

21   **JOEY:**   **So what? It's not like we're out doin' it, bozo. We're**

22   **just watchin' it. No harm in that, is there?**

23   **MARK:**   **I donno. That last one we watched, dude, I couldn't**

24   **get it out of my head. I'm sittin' in Sunday School and**

25   **it's playing up there. And it wasn't just the people in the**

26   **movie, either. People I know were in it.**

27   **JOEY:**   **So, you want me to take it back? Tell 'em, "Sorry, we**

28   **meant to rent "Bambi"?** *(Pause)*

29   **MARK:**   **No. Come on.**

30   **JOEY:**   **You sure your parents aren't going to be home?**

31   **MARK:**   **Not till tonight. Come on.**

32   **JOEY:**   **Wait. Let me stick it under my jacket.**

33   **MARK:**   **Dude, if it's so harmless, why're we hiding it?** *(They go*

34   *off. Blackout.)*

35   **VOICE:**   **Mark looked OK, but he was living a** *scary* **life!**

1   **Darkness was just around the corner. Then it happened.**
2   **One spooky Halloween night! Mark found he was turning**
3   **into . . . a zombie of the living dead!** *(A ZOMBIE comes in.*
4   *MARK screams in the darkness. Lights up. Scary and dim.*
5   *MARK is on the "bed," clutching his pillow.)*
6   **MARK: Who are you?!**
7   **ZOMBIE: I'm a zombie, dude!**
8   **MARK: Get out. Frank, is that you?**
9   **ZOMBIE: I'm all the dead stuff you do.**
10   **MARK: Take off. I don't even like their music.**
11   **ZOMBIE: You're dead, Mark.**
12   **MARK: I am not!**
13   **ZOMBIE: Inside. You're dead.**
14   **MARK: I'm alive!**
15   **ZOMBIE: Do you feel alive?**
16   **MARK:**   *(A moment)* **No.**
17   **ZOMBIE: You're a zombie, Mark. You're the living dead.**
18   **Pretty soon, everything you touch'll be dead. Then you'll**
19   **be dead. For real.**
20   **MARK: What am I supposed to do?**
21   **ZOMBIE: Before it's too late — stop living like a zombie. Stop**
22   **hanging out with zombies. Stop drinking zombies. Stop**
23   **making a zombie out of something that's supposed to be**
24   **alive.** *(The ZOMBIE leaves.)*
25   **MARK:**   *(Thrashing like in a dream)* **No, wait! Come back! I wanna**
26   **live! I wanna live!** *I wanna live!* *(The lights come up, bright.*
27   *MARK sits up in bed.)* **That was scary, kids.** *(Blackout)*
28   **VOICE:**   *(Off-stage)* **And so, not long after the freaky**
29   **Halloween night, Mark Butler's life didn't scare him ever**
30   **again. In fact, nothing scared Mark Butler.** *(Lights come*
31   *up on VANESSA, looking as before.)*
32   **VANESSA:**   *Mom, Mark's bugging me!*
33   **VOICE:**   *(Off-stage)* **Except Vanessa. But then, she could scare**
34   **Freddie Krueger.** *(Blackout)*
35

Just Be Thankful

A Sketch for Thanksgiving

PRODUCTION NOTES

This is a sketch written for the youth portion of a Thanksgiving service or as part of an all-church Thanksgiving meal.

CAST: CYNDI, a high school senior; AMBER, her little sister.

SCENE: A front room. The present.

COSTUME NOTE: Modern. Nice.

RUNNING TIME: Four to five minutes.

PROPS: Yellow notepad, pencil, dishes.

1 *AT RISE:*   Lights. CYNDI storms in with a yellow pad and a pencil.
2

3 **CYNDI:** I'm all thinking when I woke up today, great, it's
4   Thanksgiving. Load up on the bird, down ten or fifteen
5   celery sticks stuffed with peanut butter and Cheez Whiz,
6   slurp twenty olives off my fingers, a piece or two of
7   pumpkin pie — then lay around in front of the TV and
8   wish someone would've sewed my mouth closed. But no.
9   Not this year. This year I get thrown a mom curve ball.
10   This year she drops the big news, right in the middle
11   of the Macy's parade, "Cyndi, I want you to pray over the
12   meal this afternoon," she says. "I want you to find things
13   to be thankful for." I'm all, *"Mom,* what am I gonna say?
14   Everybody's gonna be here and I'll look like a geek." And
15   she goes, "Just a few things to thank God for, OK, honey?"
16   And I go, "Oh, well top'a my list is a mom who really
17   knows how to ruin a Thanksgiving meal." And she's all,
18   "Just be thankful I only ask you to do this once a year."
19   *(A creepy smile)* **Gee, thanks, Mom.** *(Pause. She writes on her*
20   *pad.)*
21   OK, number one: just be thankful she only asks me
22   to do this once a year. *(Scratches it. Sits in a huff. AMBER*
23   *walks in, carrying a stack of dishes for the table.)*
24 **AMBER:** What're you doing?
25 **CYNDI:** Mom wants me to pray over the meal this afternoon
26   and she asked me to say some things I'm thankful for.
27 **AMBER:** Oh, yeah. She asked me to do it first.
28 **CYNDI:** Why didn't you do it?
29 **AMBER:** I told her you should be the one to do it. You're
30   the oldest. *(CYNDI screams, grabs the list and writes.)*
31 **CYNDI:** "I'm thankful I'm not in prison for killing my little
32   sister."
33 **AMBER:** Geez, chill, will ya? Just say thanks for the food and
34   the sunshine and that Mom didn't mess up the yams're
35   somethin' and you're done. Easy as pie. Which reminds

1   me — I have to set the table.

2   **CYNDI:**   Siddown.

3   **AMBER:**   Excuse me?

4   **CYNDI:**   *Siddown! (AMBER sits.)*

5   **AMBER:**   What is your problem? I swear!

6   **CYNDI:**   You're gonna help me come up with stuff. *(Holds up*
7   *the pad.)* **Now, what're you thankful for?** *(Small pause)*

8   **AMBER:**   Well, I'm thankful you decided to go away to college.

9   **CYNDI:**   Come on!

10   **AMBER:**   Well, I hear it's a good school!

11   **CYNDI:**   You will wait until I actually leave before you put
12   my bed in storage, won't you?

13   **AMBER:**   Yes, but the posters come down that morning.

14   **CYNDI:**   *(A threat)* **Amber . . .**

15   **AMBER:**   OK, OK. *(Pause)* **I'm thankful we have Mom.**

16   **CYNDI:**   *(Writing)* **Yeah. That's right.**

17   **AMBER:**   And that Dad was here as long as he was.

18   **CYNDI:**   That's right. And I'm thankful we have food on the
19   table.

20   **AMBER:**   I'll bet you are.

21   **CYNDI:**   *(Ignoring her)* **And that we have people to enjoy it**
22   with.

23   **AMBER:**   Although you seem to enjoy it all by yourself.

24   **CYNDI:**   I'm thankful my sister's so funny.

25   **AMBER:**   *(Rolling her eyes)* **Yeah, right.**

26   **CYNDI:**   *(Serious)* **Yeah, right.** *(Pause)*

27   **AMBER:**   Get outta Dodge.

28   **CYNDI:**   I mean it. Laughing with you has helped a lot,
29   Amber. A whole lot. I remember some of those nights
30   when we sat up all night laughing into our pillows and
31   Mom screaming from her bedroom to shut up.

32   **AMBER:**   Ah, you're an easy mark.

33   **CYNDI:**   Thanks.

34   **AMBER:**   Don't mention it. Come to think of it, I kinda liked
35   making you laugh.

1   **CYNDI:**   Ah, I just let ya.

2   **AMBER:**   Thanks.

3   **CYNDI:**   Don't mention it. You know, it just hit me — this is

4   going to be my last Thanksgiving at home before I go off

5   to school.

6   **AMBER:**   I hate you. When you come back you're going to get

7   to sit at the big table. You're not gonna have to wait for

8   a handout to get something to eat.

9   **CYNDI:**   Well, I could just stay here and go to city college.

10   **AMBER:**   Write down, "I'm thankful my little sister didn't

11   shove a yam up my nose on my last Thanksgiving at

12   home."

13   **CYNDI:**   *(Writing)* "I'm glad my little sister was here on my

14   last Thanksgiving at home."

15   **AMBER:**   Yeah. And don't you forget it.

16   **CYNDI:**   Just set the table.

17   **AMBER:**   *(As she goes off)* Oh, sure, I gotta do manual labor

18   while you getta sit around on her size nine/ten being

19   thankful.

20   **CYNDI:**   *(Calling after her)* That's cuz I'm the oldest! *(Pause.*

21   *She writes.)* "I'm also glad olives are the perfect size to fit

22   on your fingers." *(Blackout)*

23

24

25

26

27

28

29

30

31

32

33

34

35

Mall Medley

A Sketch for Christmas

PRODUCTION NOTES

Mall Medley was written to be used in conjunction with a junior high or high school caroling event in the mall or an outside program.

The three sketches can be done with carols or separately.

CAST: CAROLERS; DUDE 1; DUDE 2; CRAZED TEEN, BRIEL, an angel.

SCENE: A mall. The present.

COSTUME NOTE: Modern.

RUNNING TIME: Twelve to fifteen minutes.

PROPS: Signs, Christmas list, flashlight, a stool or bench.

1   *AT RISE:*   A group of CAROLERS (youth choir) in a mall or on a
2   street corner. They begin with "Joy to the World," then "O Little
3   Town of Bethlehem." DUDE 1 and DUDE 2 come out from the
4   choir. The CAROLERS hold up signs with store names on them.
5
6   **DUDE 1:**   *(See DUDE 2)* **Dude!**
7   **DUDE 2:**   **Dude!** *(They shake hands.)*
8   **DUDE 1:**   **So what's up?**
9   **DUDE 2:**   **Just here for the hang. What're you doin'?**
10   **DUDE 1:**   **The same.**
11   **DUDE 2:**   **Cool.** *(They both mime watching a girl walk by.)* **Babe-a-**
12   **lonia.** *(Calling after her)* **Hey, you have yerself a merry**
13   **little Christmas, OK?**
14   **DUDE 1:**   **All right.**
15   **DUDE 2:**   **So, how's yer Christmas goin'?**
16   **DUDE 1:**   **Excellent. What about yours?**
17   **DUDE 2:**   **Bonus. It's a total party, man. I'm all in the spirit**
18   **and all.**
19   **DUDE 1:**   **All right.**
20   **DUDE 2:**   **All right.** *(They mime watching someone walk by. They're*
21   *astonished.)* **Whoa. Was that Mrs. Michaels from American**
22   **History class?**
23   **DUDE 1:**   **No doubt.**
24   **DUDE 2:**   **Sure looks different when she's not like standing**
25   **in front of a chalkboard and stuff.**
26   **DUDE 1:**   **Absolutely.**
27   **DUDE 2:**   *(Looking off)* **Dude, check it out, isn't that yer mom**
28   **over there?**
29   **DUDE 1:**   *(Ignoring her)* **Get out.**
30   **DUDE 2:**   **Dude, she's over there. Wavin' at you and all.**
31   *(Laughs)* **She's hacked, man. Her eyes are like bulgin' out**
32   **of her head. Whoa, I think it's time for you to go home.**
33   **DUDE 1:**   **I told her I didn't wanna go Christmas shoppin'**
34   **with her. Parents are so wasted, man. They're so**
35   **embarrassing to have around.**

1	DUDE 2:	Tell me about it.
2	DUDE 1:	*(Looks off at mom)* **All right!** *(Turns back.)* **I'll see ya.**
3	DUDE 2:	Later.
4	DUDE 1:	So, what're you doin' for Christmas, anyways?
5	DUDE 2:	Celebrating right here.
6	DUDE 1:	In the mall?

7 DUDE 2: Where else? It's got everything I need. If I can't find
8 it in the mall, dude, I don't need it. *(Pointing off)* Hey, she's
9 freakin', man. You better hustle it. And don't look in those
10 bags. Looks like she bought a lotta neat stuff for ya.
11 DUDE 1: Parents, dude. I wish they were invisible. *(DUDE 1*
12 *walks away.)*
13 DUDE 2: *(Sadly)* Yeah. Tell me about it. *(He sits. Drops his head*
14 *in his hands.)*
15 *(The CAROLERS sing "O Come, All Ye Faithful," followed*
16 *by "It Came Upon the Midnight Clear," and closing with "What*
17 *Child Is This?" At the close of the song, the CAROLERS hold*
18 *up signs that read, "Christmas Sale!" "Half Price!" "Give*
19 *Something Special for Christmas," etc. CRAZED TEEN steps*
20 *out of the CAROLERS, frantically looking over a Christmas list.)*
21 CRAZED TEEN: That's it. I'm waxed. Totally blown out. I've
22 got twenty people on my list and enough cash for about
23 half of 'em. Man, Christmas was coming. I knew it, too. I
24 should have taken that extra part-time job. I should have
25 put the hours in and made some major cash while I had
26 the chance. So who cares if I flunk out of high school?
27 College can wait. This is Christmas we're talking about.
28 If I don't buy great stuff, I look like the cheapest dweeb
29 in town. *(Checks the list.)*
30 Well, I'm going to have to lose half these people.
31 What else can I do? But who? I mean, my family, I can't
32 blow them off. Maybe my little brother. Naw, he'd have
33 a cow. Wait ... Grandma. Yeah. She always gives me a
34 stupid card with five bucks in it. It's been the same
35 amount since I was eight. Who needs it? *(Scratches the list.)*

1 You're history, Grandma. OK, OK. I'm on a roll.
2 Lessee ... Mark and Tiffany. Are they gonna ... naw,
3 they're not gonna get me anything. Total tightwads.
4 *(Scratches them.)* Later, dudes. Yeah, I better get Joel
5 something. That is, *if* I want to see the light of prom night.
6 And Uncle Yuke and Aunt Fanny? Every year I get the
7 free make-up they get when they buy something great
8 for someone else. *(Scratches)* Crash and burn. *(Big scratch)*
9 OK, from here down on the list, hasta la bye-bye. *(Tears*
10 *the list in half.)*
11   What else can I do? Man, I get more nervous around
12 Christmas than I do before my geometry exam. *(To the*
13 *audience)* That sound right to you? That the way it's
14 supposed to be? You know, when I didn't have any money
15 at all, I used to make cards and stuff for people. Glitter
16 and glue and construction paper. Tell 'em I loved 'em and
17 all. They seemed happy with that. Now ... *(Pause)* I wish
18 I was one'a those wise men, y'know? They had it made.
19 They only had to buy for one. *(Looks at watch.)* The mall's
20 closing! Ten more people! *(CRAZED TEEN runs off.)*
21   *(The CAROLERS sing "We Three Kings of Orient Are"*
22 *and "The First Noel." At the close of the carol, BRIEL comes out*
23 *and sits on a high stool or bench. She's wearing white and carries*
24 *a large, wide-beam flashlight. She looks down as if from way*
25 *up on high.)*
26 BRIEL: Look at 'em, all down there! Running around,
27 climbing the walls, looking for that one thing that'll make
28 their lives bright. Well, they don't really know what
29 bright is, lemme tell you. But they'll know soon enough.
30 *(Sighs. Thinks.)* I donno. This whole manger idea. You
31 think it's too light a touch? Too simple ... or not ... y'know,
32 big enough? I mean, it's so hectic down there, I wonder
33 if Bethlehem and a bunch of cold, sleepy shepherds is
34 even gonna get any notice? Might get ... lost in the
35 shuffle, y'know? You think? I donno. One thing I can say,

1   it's something completely different. I'll bet no one
2   thought it would all happen like this! It's very . . . well,
3   human, y'know. A stable, smelly animals, a young girl in
4   labor. God's comin' in . . . well, a little on the earthy side,
5   if you ask me. But I like the idea. *(Looks down. Smiles.)*
6   Those half-asleep shepherds are never gonna know what
7   hit 'em. Half asleep! What am I talking about? It's time
8   to move! *(Stands up and switches on the flashlight, shining it*
9   *down like a spotlight.)*
10   Don't be afraid! I'm bringing you good news of great
11 joy which'll be for all people! Tonight in Bethlehem, a
12 Savior's been born to you! *(BRIEL freezes.)*
13   *(The CAROLERS immediately sing, "Hark, the Herald*
14 *Angels Sing!" BRIEL then joins the other singers for "Angels*
15 *We Have Heard on High," "Silent Night," and "We Wish You a*
16 *Merry Christmas.")*
17
18
19
20
21
22
23
24
25
26
27
28
29
30
31
32
33
34
35

Gedda Life!

A Sketch for New Year's

Ben Winter in *Gedda Life!*.

PRODUCTION NOTES

We wrote *Gedda Life!* to be used for a New Year's talk or discussion on how Jesus can change our life's course, instill self-esteem and offer courage.

The sketch was written from the perspective of an unbeliever.

It's important to stress that, unlike the instant change the world offers on the outside, the change brought on the inside by Christ is at once miraculously immediate, and graciously lifelong.

CAST: SAM, a high schooler.

SCENE: A front room. The present.

COSTUME NOTE: Modern.

RUNNING TIME: Three to four minutes.

PROPS: Table, chair, party hat, "Happy New Year" sign, party favor, confetti, yellow notepad, radio.

1 *AT RISE:*   Lights. SAM sits at a table with a party hat, favor, a
2 yellow notepad, and a pile of confetti. A sign behind him reads,
3 "Happy New Year!" The radio on the table is blasting the Top
4 Forty Countdown. SAM is rocking. Notices the audience. Turns
5 down the radio.)
6
7 **SAM: Last New Year's I made a vow that by this year I was**
8 **going to look just like Arnold Schwarzenegger.** *(Looks at*
9 *himself.)* **I could've done it, too, except I . . . well I had a**
10 **lot of homework. And I sprained my wrist playing**
11 **badminton, so I couldn't push the big ones anymore. It's**
12 **a drag, too. I was getting pretty buff there. Course it's**
13 **fading now. Not too much, though. I mean, I could get it**
14 **back, with a good pump or two. Really.** *(Small pause)*
15   **All right, I'll level with ya. I couldn't hang with the**
16 **Schwarzenegger routine. The workouts and the eating**
17 **raw eggs and the protein powder and doin' the**
18 **Stairmaster and all. You ever tried the Stairmaster?**
19 **Thing'll kill ya. So I gave up. I just bagged the burn and**
20 **went for Haagen Daz and sleeping in late. And now I'm**
21 **back to me again. Just me. Nothing special. Nothing**
22 **extraordinary. Nothing anybody's gonna take a second**
23 **look at. Another year of nothing changing. Even if I try.**
24 *(Blows the blower and throws a handful of confetti in the air.)*
25   **But that's the problem, y'see. I wanna change. I don't**
26 **wanna be me anymore. I don't like me. Nobody likes me.**
27 **So I've got this list of stuff I wanna make my New Year's**
28 **resolutions. Well, here it is.** *(Reads)* **I wanna stop being**
29 **so afraid. Man, I'd rather blow off class than walk in a**
30 **minute late and have everybody stare at me. I wanna**
31 **stop letting what other people say bother me. Who cares**
32 **what anybody thinks, right? Twenty years from now they**
33 **gonna be around? I wanna start enjoying my life. I wanna**
34 **start taking chances. I wanna start thinking I'm worth**
35 **something. I wanna stop feeling so rotten about myself.**

I wanna feel like I'm on this planet for a reason. I wanna stop hating myself. I wanna start, y'know . . . living for a change. *(Puts down the list. Takes a deep breath.)*

Well, nothing major. Just a few changes here and there. You know, I tried making all these changes out here. Really, I was getting buff there for awhile. And I went to this tanning salon for a few weeks. But I still hated myself. So who cares? Doesn't take long before I'm not lookin' at what's in the T-shirt, but what's behind the eyes. Surprise. It's still me. *(Puts on the hat, picks up the favor and a handful of confetti.)*

So, that's it. My New Year's resolution. By this time next year, I vow to become a totally new person! Out with the old, in with the new! I'm going to gedda life! *(Toots the favor, throws the confetti.)*

OK . . . so does anybody know where I'm supposed to start? *(The lights fade to blackout.)*

Hope He's Not Up Yet

A Sketch for Easter

Rachel Down (L), Lauren Down in *Hope He's Not Up Yet*.

PRODUCTION NOTES

This sketch was written to illustrate God's forgiving power, even when we fail miserably. The Father waits at the door to let us in.

This was designed for Easter, but with some careful editing, you can make this a year 'round piece.

CAST: LAUREN, sixteen or so; KIRK, a junior higher; DAD, an adult.

SCENE: A front door. The present.

COSTUME NOTE: Modern.

RUNNING TIME: Five minutes.

PROPS: Door frame, steps, newspaper, Walkman.

1 *AT RISE:*   A front porch. A set of steps leading up to a door frame.
2   Just before dawn. Unbelievably quiet. Suddenly, rock or rap
3   music at major decibels. LAUREN walks in, headphones on,
4   tape in forward motion. She's rocking as she walks, oblivious
5   to where she is. LAUREN is sixteen or so, still drunk right now.
6   She looks up and sees the front door. She stops. She takes off
7   the earphones. The music stops immediately. She snaps off the
8   tape, lets the phones hang around her neck. Stares at the door.
9

10 **LAUREN:**   **Hope he's not up yet. If he is, I'm tofu, man.** *(Checks*
11   *her watch.)* **You're kidding me! It can't be 5:30 a.m.! Mark**
12   **told me it was 3 a.m. when I left his house. What a dork.**
13   *(Louder. To the front door)* **Well, if you'd'a given me a car**
14   **like I asked, I'd'a been home two hours ago.** *(Stares at the*
15   *door.)* **Lauren, if you walk in there now, you'd better be**
16   **ready to —**
17 **OFF-STAGE VOICE:** *Loook ooouuut! (A newspaper comes*
18   *sailing in. LAUREN ducks. It lands on the steps. LAUREN*
19   *grabs it and goes to throw it at Off-stage delivery person.)*
20 **LAUREN:**   *(Yelling off)* **You want me to cut off your**
21   **circulation?!** *(Sees the front page. Reads:)*
22   **"Happy Easter"?** *(Unfolds the paper.)* **No way. Oh,**
23   **that's just great. It's Easter morning. I totally spaced it.**
24   **That means I came in from partying at 5:30 a.m. on Easter**
25   **morning. Well, no Easter Egg hunt for me, that's for total**
26   **sure. Ah, man. I'm dead meat. I'm totally wasted. I mean,**
27   **I'm even *more* wasted.** *(Looks up at the door.)* **He's gonna**
28   **kill me. This is the biggest dork head move of 'em all.**
29   **He's gonna nail me to the wall. For life.** *(Shakes her head.)*
30   **Easter morning.** *(Looks up at the door.)* **I wonder if he's up**
31   **yet. If he's not, I gotta chance.** *(Small pause. She goes to her*
32   *"bedroom window" and tries to open it. It's locked.)*
33   **No way! I unlocked my bedroom window before I**
34   **left. Incredible. My own father locked me out. That's low.**
35   **Way low. Locking his own daughter out. The dork.** *(She*

1   *sits down on the steps. Feels in her pockets and finds a half-pint*
2   *bottle of Jack Daniels. Goes to drink. It's empty. She slings it.)*
3   **OK, I'll just lie out here and freeze to death. That'll make**
4   **'im feel great. Lockin' the door on me.** *(Lies back on the*
5   *steps. Pulls her headphones on. Sudden loud music. KIRK,*
6   *LAUREN's younger brother, comes around the corner of the*
7   *house. He's in his bathrobe and slippers. He sees LAUREN lying*
8   *on the steps and freaks out. Thinks she's dead.)*
9   **KIRK:**   **Lauren? Lauren!** *(Runs to her and starts shaking her.)*
10   **Lauren, get up!** *Lauren, get up!* *(LAUREN sits up, freaked*
11   *out. She pulls her earphones off. Sudden quiet.)*
12   **LAUREN:**   **What're you doin'! Scared me to death!**
13   **KIRK:**   *(Catching his breath)* **I . . . I thought you . . .**
14   **LAUREN:**   **What?!**
15   **KIRK:**   **I thought you were dead, OK?**
16   **LAUREN:**   *(Moans)* **I feel like I'm dead. My head's spinning.** *(A*
17   *deep breath.)* **Don't throw up. Don't. I can handle it. Handle**
18   **it.**
19   **KIRK:**   **You know it's Easter?**
20   **LAUREN:**   **Hey, I read the papers.**
21   **KIRK:**   **You wasted?** *(Beat)* **Lauren, would you tell me what's**
22   **happening to you?**
23   **LAUREN:**   **That's nunya.**
24   **KIRK:**   **What?**
25   **LAUREN: Nunya business. Go on back to bed, geek.**
26   **KIRK:**   **He told me to tell 'im if I heard you.**
27   **LAUREN:**   **So go tell 'im.** *(Small pause)*
28   **KIRK:**   **I think he knows.** *(KIRK sits down.)* **You're scaring**
29   **me.**
30   **LAUREN:**   *(Laughs)* **I'm scaring you?**
31   **KIRK:**   **Why are you so ticked off all the time?**
32   **LAUREN:**   **I'm not. It's just that everybody around is so**
33   **goldarned happy all the time, I look ticked off.** *(Pause)*
34   **KIRK:**   **You look terrible.**
35   **LAUREN:**   **I feel like I'm dead.**

1 KIRK: So partying till 5 in the morning makes you feel more
2   alive?
3 LAUREN: *(A lie)* **Totally more.**
4 KIRK: I don't believe you.
5 LAUREN: Why not, Kirkie?
6 KIRK: Because you said that the same way you promised me
7   you weren't the one who hung my dirty underwear in
8   my locker.
9 LAUREN: *(A lie)* I didn't. Look, I need to get some sleep, OK,
10   before he gets up and wails on me. I'm gonna need my
11   strength.
12 KIRK: Why doncha just go in?
13 LAUREN: I want 'im to find me out here, frozen stiff, so he'll
14   feel like a total dork. Man, I feel like garbage.
15 KIRK: You can't try to sneak in anyway. I locked your
16   bedroom window.
17 LAUREN: You what?
18 KIRK: You gonna try and sneak in? Get out. You don't think
19   he knows you been gone all night? What kind'a dad you
20   think we got? *(Pause)* Look, he worried about you all night
21   'n I just didn't want you sneaking in without him finding
22   out.
23 LAUREN: After all I've done for you.
24 KIRK: He was freaked out, man! You should'a seen him. You
25   don't see him cuz you take off and I see how he feels
26   when you don't come back, or you come back all wasted.
27   You deserve to get it big time, that's all I gotta say.
28 LAUREN: Well it doesn't matter what you got to say.
29 KIRK: That's what I told him. I told him to give it to you good.
30   I said, "Man, you're gonna kill 'er, aren't you Dad?" And
31   he said, "I think she's doin' a pretty good job of that
32   herself."
33 LAUREN: You're full of it. He didn't say that.
34 KIRK: Uh-huh. He said what she's doin' to herself is punish-
35   ment enough.

1   LAUREN: What does he know about it? The dork.
2   KIRK: He said he's been there.
3   LAUREN: Nobody's been here!
4   KIRK: He has. *(A beat)* Lauren, is this, like, a dysfunctional
5   family system thing?
6   LAUREN: A what?
7   KIRK: I read about it in "People" magazine.
8   LAUREN: Get out. I need to get some sleep.
9   KIRK: Why doncha just go in?
10 LAUREN: Because the door's locked, doofus.
11 KIRK: No it's not.
12 LAUREN: Of course it is! He locked me out! He's ticked off!
13   *(Pause)* You mean, it's been open all this time? *(KIRK nods.)*
14   I figured he'd'a locked me out.
15 KIRK: Why would he do that to you?
16 LAUREN: Because I'm not the sweet little girl he thought I
17   was, that's why! *(Pause)* I failed him. *(The door opens. Inside*
18   *light cuts down the steps and hits LAUREN. She stands. DAD*
19   *comes out on the doorstep. He's dressed. Never went to bed.*
20   *Pause.)*
21 LAUREN: Daddy?
22 DAD: Why didn't you come in?
23 LAUREN: I thought you locked the door.
24 DAD: I left it open. Didn't you try it? *(LAUREN shakes her*
25   *head.)* You wanna come in?
26 LAUREN: I'm still drunk.
27 DAD: Come on.
28 KIRK: I can't believe this. You're not gonna wail on her? I
29   know, I know. She's wailed on herself enough already.
30   What happens if I came home wasted at 5 a.m. on Easter
31   morning?
32 DAD: You wouldn't. You've got different problems, Kirk. Not
33   like your sister's. *(Beat)* And I'd leave the door open for
34   you if you did. But don't. *(Pause)* Come on in, you two. *(Pause.*
35   *LAUREN goes up the stairs. Looks at her DAD. Passes him and*

1 *goes inside.)*
2 **KIRK:** **Unbelievable. You are unbelievable.** *(Small pause)*
3 **DAD:** **I hope not.** *(Blackout)*
4
5
6
7
8
9
10
11
12
13
14
15
16
17
18
19
20
21
22
23
24
25
26
27
28
29
30
31
32
33
34
35

ABOUT THE AUTHORS

Photo: Debra Classen

Lawrence and Annie Enscoe have written twelve theatre-related books, either separately or together. They are the authors of *Joy to the World,* a popular book of Christmas plays. They wrote a best-selling book of teen issue plays which garnered the Angel Award. The plays have been praised and produced by church and secular groups alike. They are also the authors of *Pew Prompters* and contributed to a teen collection called *Skits-O-Phrenia.*

Lawrence has written three previous play collections which have been performed on stages and sanctuary platforms from coast to coast and abroad.

The Enscoes make their home in Pasadena, where they are full-time screenwriters. Lawrence studied dramatic arts at Westmont College and the University of California (Berkeley). He was formerly an entertainment writer for the *Los Angeles Daily News.* Annie studied education and theatre at Wheaton College. She has taught drama in both classroom and seminar settings.

You'll want to check out these additional sketches:

THE BEST OF THE JEREMIAH PEOPLE

by
Jim Custer and
Bob Hoose

GET A GRIP! has brought out the entertainers in your youth group. Now they want to perform more sketches — on Sunday mornings, at retreats, camps, youth group meetings, Youth Sunday and other occasions. What better place to continue your drama ministry than with a book by America's leading Christian repertory group? **THE BEST OF THE JEREMIAH PEOPLE** is chock full of the group's trademark warm and forgiving satire with a "stinger" at the end. All sketches have been performance-tested through the Jeremiah People's twenty-plus successful years of touring nationwide. They also share their experience on rehearsing, theatre games, forms to help you set up a drama ministry, blocking, and managing lighting and sound on a budget.

Sample sketch titles include:

"A Typical Drive to Work?"

"Call Me Any Time"

"$685.00 Air Filter"

As with **GET A GRIP!**, performance rights and permission to reproduce the sketches for your group are included with purchase of the book. This paperback is available at your local Christian bookstore or directly from the publisher: **Meriwether Publishing Ltd., P.O. Box 7710, Colorado Springs, CO 80933.**

ORDER FORM

MERIWETHER PUBLISHING LTD.
P.O. BOX 7710
COLORADO SPRINGS, CO 80933
TELEPHONE: (719) 594-4422

Please send me the following books:

_____ **Get a Grip! #CC-B128** $10.95
by L. G. Enscoe and Annie Enscoe
Contemporary scenes and monologs for Christian teens

_____ **Joy to the World! #CC-B161** $12.95
by L. G. Enscoe and Annie Enscoe
A variety collection of Christmas programs

_____ **The Best of the Jeremiah People #CC-B117** $14.95
by Jim Custer and Bob Hoose
Humorous skits and sketches by leading Christian repertory group

_____ **Divine Comedies #CC-B190** $12.95
by T. M. Williams
A collection of plays for church drama groups

_____ **Sermons Alive! #CC-B132** $12.95
by Paul Neale Lessard
52 dramatic sketches for worship services

_____ **Teaching With Bible Games #CC-B108** $10.95
by Ed Dunlop
20 "kid-tested" contests for Christian education

_____ **The Clown Ministry Handbook #CC-B163** $10.95
by Janet Litherland
The first and most complete text on the art of clown ministry

These and other fine Meriwether Publishing books are available
at your local Christian bookstore or direct from the publisher. Use
the handy order form on this page.

NAME: _____

ORGANIZATION NAME: _____

ADDRESS: _____

CITY:_____ STATE: _____ ZIP: _____

PHONE: _____
❏ **Check Enclosed**
❏ **Visa or MasterCard #** _____
                                              Expiration
Signature: _____ *Date:* _____
            (required for Visa/MasterCard orders)

COLORADO RESIDENTS: Please add 3% sales tax.
SHIPPING: Include $2.75 for the first book and 50¢ for each additional book ordered.

❏ *Please send me a copy of your complete catalog of books and plays.*

ORDER FORM

MERIWETHER PUBLISHING LTD.
P.O. BOX 7710
COLORADO SPRINGS, CO 80933
TELEPHONE: (719) 594-4422

Please send me the following books:

_____ **Get a Grip! #CC-B128**   **$10.95**
  by L. G. Enscoe and Annie Enscoe
  Contemporary scenes and monologs for Christian teens

_____ **Joy to the World! #CC-B161**   **$12.95**
  by L. G. Enscoe and Annie Enscoe
  A variety collection of Christmas programs

_____ **The Best of the Jeremiah People #CC-B117**   **$14.95**
  by Jim Custer and Bob Hoose
  Humorous skits and sketches by leading Christian repertory group

_____ **Divine Comedies #CC-B190**   **$12.95**
  by T. M. Williams
  A collection of plays for church drama groups

_____ **Sermons Alive! #CC-B132**   **$12.95**
  by Paul Neale Lessard
  52 dramatic sketches for worship services

_____ **Teaching With Bible Games #CC-B108**   **$10.95**
  by Ed Dunlop
  20 "kid-tested" contests for Christian education

_____ **The Clown Ministry Handbook #CC-B163**   **$10.95**
  by Janet Litherland
  The first and most complete text on the art of clown ministry

These and other fine Meriwether Publishing books are available
at your local Christian bookstore or direct from the publisher. Use
the handy order form on this page.

NAME: _____

ORGANIZATION NAME: _____

ADDRESS: _____

CITY:_____ STATE: _____ ZIP: _____

PHONE: _____
  ❑ **Check Enclosed**
  ❑ **Visa or MasterCard #** _____
                                    Expiration
Signature: _____   *Date:* _____
      (required for Visa/MasterCard orders)

COLORADO RESIDENTS: Please add 3% sales tax.
SHIPPING: Include $2.75 for the first book and 50¢ for each additional book ordered.

  ❑ *Please send me a copy of your complete catalog of books and plays.*

ORDER FORM

MERIWETHER PUBLISHING LTD.
P.O. BOX 7710
COLORADO SPRINGS, CO 80933
TELEPHONE: (719) 594-4422

Please send me the following books:

_____ **Get a Grip! #CC-B128**   **$10.95**
by L. G. Enscoe and Annie Enscoe
Contemporary scenes and monologs for Christian teens

_____ **Joy to the World! #CC-B161**   **$12.95**
by L. G. Enscoe and Annie Enscoe
A variety collection of Christmas programs

_____ **The Best of the Jeremiah People #CC-B117**   **$14.95**
by Jim Custer and Bob Hoose
Humorous skits and sketches by leading Christian repertory group

_____ **Divine Comedies #CC-B190**   **$12.95**
by T. M. Williams
A collection of plays for church drama groups

_____ **Sermons Alive! #CC-B132**   **$12.95**
by Paul Neale Lessard
52 dramatic sketches for worship services

_____ **Teaching With Bible Games #CC-B108**   **$10.95**
by Ed Dunlop
20 "kid-tested" contests for Christian education

_____ **The Clown Ministry Handbook #CC-B163**   **$10.95**
by Janet Litherland
The first and most complete text on the art of clown ministry

**These and other fine Meriwether Publishing books are available
at your local Christian bookstore or direct from the publisher. Use
the handy order form on this page.**

NAME: _____

ORGANIZATION NAME: _____

ADDRESS: _____

CITY:_____ STATE: _____ ZIP: _____

PHONE: _____
  ❏ **Check Enclosed**
  ❏ **Visa or MasterCard #** _____
                                                    Expiration
Signature: _____ *Date:* _____
              (required for Visa/MasterCard orders)

COLORADO RESIDENTS: Please add 3% sales tax.
SHIPPING: Include $2.75 for the first book and 50¢ for each additional book ordered.

  ❏ *Please send me a copy of your complete catalog of books and plays.*